AFRICAN TEXTILES AND DECORATIVE ARTS

BY ROY SIEBER

THE MUSEUM
OF MODERN ART
NEW YORK

SCHEDULE OF THE EXHIBITION
The Museum of Modern Art, New York, October 11, 1972–January 31, 1973
Los Angeles County Museum of Art, March 20–May 31, 1973
M. H. de Young Memorial Museum, San Francisco, July 2–August 31, 1973
The Cleveland Museum of Art, October 3–December 2, 1973

Library of Congress Catalog Card Number 72-76268
Paperbound ISBN 0-87070-227-0
Cloth binding ISBN 0-87070-228-9
Designed by Carl Laanes
Type set by Boro Typographers, Inc., New York
Printed by Eastern Press, Inc., New Haven, Connecticut
Bound by A. Horowitz & Son, Bookbinders, Clifton, New Jersey
The Museum of Modern Art
11 West 53 Street, New York, New York 10019
Printed in the United States of America

CONTENTS

ACKNOWLEDGMENTS

Many people have been generous in their assistance in the preparation of this book and the exhibition it accompanies. I wish to express my gratitude to The Museum of Modern Art and to Arthur Drexler, Director of the Museum's Department of Architecture and Design, for the invitation to direct this exhibition. I must thank particularly Mrs. Katherine White Reswick of The International Council of The Museum of Modern Art for her efforts in helping to prepare it. Soon after preliminary plans were made, Mrs. Reswick volunteered to make a survey of African textiles and jewelry in American collections. This quickly became a voyage of discovery, for museums and private collections revealed a totally unexpected wealth of examples. In the course of her survey, she traveled 75,000 miles to visit twenty-three public institutions and fifty-seven private collections, photographing over 2,400 works during her travels. These constitute an archive of great value for the study of African crafts. From this survey a selection was made for the exhibition and for illustration here.

In making that selection, Arthur Drexler brought his perceptive and discriminating eye to bear on the multitude of works, and with Mrs. Reswick and Roslyn Walker Randall aided me in making those final difficult judgments necessary to such a selection. I learned more than a little in those sessions.

I would like to acknowledge my debt to The Ford Foundation, Indiana University, and the African Studies Institutes of the University of Ghana and the University of Ife in Nigeria for making possible various research trips to Africa between 1958 and 1971, all of which have contributed to my ever-growing interest in African crafts. Further, particular acknowledgment must be made to the National Endowment for the Humanities in Washington, D.C., for its support of my specialized study of textiles and other crafts in Nigeria in 1971. On that trip, His Excellency the Timi of Ede and Chief Longe were most helpful.

I would also like to express my gratitude to Mrs. Constance Work and Miss Geneva Warner of the Lilly Rare Books Library at Indiana University for their invaluable help in my search for early travelers' accounts of African textiles and decorative arts. Alma Eikerman, Terry Illes, Budd Stalnaker, and Joan Sterrenberg of the Faculty of the Fine Arts Department of Indiana University were most patient and helpful with technical problems.

Grateful acknowledgment is made to the many museums and

private collectors who have allowed their works to be reproduced here. Through the kind intervention of Donald Morris, Jeanne Rucquoi Berger most generously made available a series of photographs, "L'Afrique qui disparait," obtained in the Congo about thirty years ago by her father. Several have been included among the illustrations for this book.

The staff of The Museum of Modern Art has been most helpful in preparations for both book and exhibition. Kathryn Eno of the Department of Architecture and Design has been unfailing in her efforts to gather photographs for this book and to execute details of the exhibition. Jane Fluegel, Associate Editor in the Department of Publications, has shepherded my book through publication. Jean-Edith Weiffenbach, Senior Cataloguer in the Department of the Registrar, has overcome the many difficulties involved in assembling works for the exhibition.

During the preparation of this book, I learned of the death of Frances S. Herskovits, who, with her husband, the late Melville J. Herskovits, were pioneers in African studies in this country. With wit and imagination they led me to discover the rich delights of African culture. This book is fondly dedicated to their memory.

In the essay that follows, an attempt has been made to keep specialized terms and technical jargon to a minimum. The notes and bibliographic references to technical processes should aid the interested reader in finding more complete descriptions of those processes. All costumes, jewelry, and textiles illustrated, excepting those in field photographs, appear in the exhibition at The Museum of Modern Art. I have tried to provide in each caption a reference to the culture, the specific village location (if known), and the country of origin of each piece. Few examples can be dated with real accuracy, for collectors rarely inquire after such details. Where the date of collection is known, it is given. In general, however, it is safe to assume that the examples are of recent fabrication.

Roy Sieber, Guest Director of the Exhibition

This book and the exhibition it accompanies
have been prepared under the auspices of
The International Council of The Museum of Modern Art, New York,
and have been made possible by
the generous assistance and support of the
National Endowment for the Arts in Washington, D.C.,
a Federal agency,
and of Exxon Corporation.

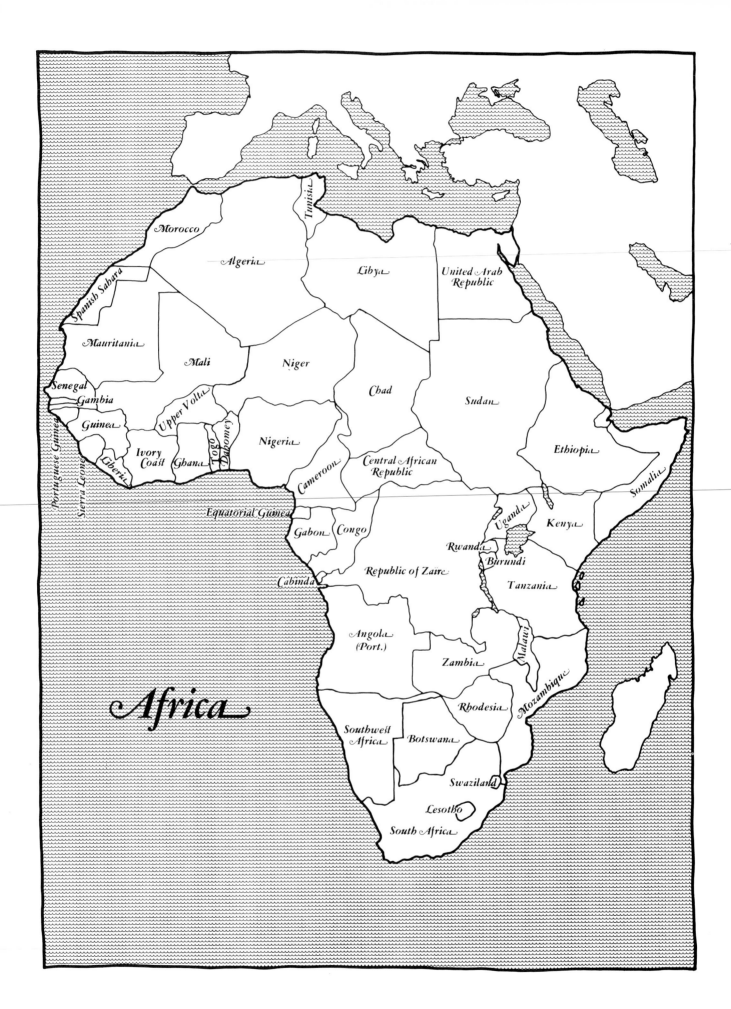

Africa

AFRICAN TEXTILES AND DECORATIVE ARTS

TOGETHER this essay and its illustrations constitute an introduction to the rich and varied world of African textiles and decorative arts, particularly costumes and jewelry. The study of these traditional forms has been neglected by the West, where attention has been focused primarily on the sculpture of Africa. This attitude not only stems from Western aesthetic values but results in a geographical emphasis on West Africa where most traditional sculpture is to be found. However, the richness of invention and variety in the arts of personal adornment is *pan*-African and may, indeed, reveal the breadth and range of the aesthetic life of traditional Africa with greater accuracy than the limited formulations that currently serve in the West as a basis for most studies in African art.

Africa has a far greater variety of textiles, jewelry, and other arts of adornment than can here be sampled. An attempt has been made in this volume to ferret out what seems most exciting. At the same time a general survey is intended: no style or geographical area of sub-Saharan Africa has been consciously ignored, although some have had to be omitted for want of space or availability. Further, an attempt has been made to demonstrate the range of costumes, jewelry, and textiles, to juxtapose the casual, or even inconsequential—but delightful—object with the awesome, even pompous, panoply of leadership: a poor man's shirt with a king's tunic; necklaces of beetle-wing covers with necklaces of gold.

Nearly all of the objects have been produced within the last century; many are recent, and some are new. Almost all represent technical processes that are still in use and reflect contemporary African taste.

A recent and growing literature of African crafts seems strongest perhaps for textiles, weaker for jewelry, and indifferent for those crafts such as pottery, which are not here represented. The bibliography prepared by Roslyn Walker Randall makes reference to these studies, as well as to writings of ethnographers and other observors. Her compilation is intended to take the interested reader further than this essay would allow.

The literature of African arts has tended to deal with their "traditional" aspects, implying that as they have become "modern"—that is, as they have come increasingly under the influence of outside factors—they have lost an irreplaceable élan. Actually, of course, African art is no more frozen in time than the art of any other society. The Western world has no monopoly on history. The flow of change in time is as real in Africa as anywhere else; internal and external forces have modified societies and their arts so that each object may be viewed as the end point of a historical development.

Yet, the data for historical changes are thin, in part because we have failed to seek the evidence. Thus, for the moment, we must deal with the objects of adornment and apparel not as timeless but as historically untamed.

The geographical boundaries of the works examined include all of sub-Saharan Africa—Black Africa—not because this was a hermetically sealed unit but because the emphases of history are significantly different for the north. The historical axes for Egypt, the Classical world, Islam, and the Coptic world are the Mediterranean, the Levant, and the Near East. Through trade they have influenced Africa south to the Sahara but have been little influenced in return.

Where the impact of interior or exterior forces of change seems clear, those forces are noted. Thus we have endeavored to indicate the impact of the West and of Islam or at least have not rigorously avoided indicating such influences. It is fascinating to note that European influences tend to replace traditional forms and values; Islamic influences, in sharp contrast, tend to augment traditional aesthetic values. Just as Islamic religious activities in Africa tend toward syncretisms and adjustment, Christianity tends toward displacement and substitution. Thus, more often than not, we find *things* from Europe and *techniques* from Islam: beads and cloths from Europe; silversmithing forms and looms from the east and north.

Thus, it is neither an aim nor, more realistically, is it possible, in the light of present evidence, to present a firm, clear history of African costume, body decoration, jewelry, and textiles. Where possible, historical notes are given, these gleaned from early travelers' reports. It is startling to discover that for about three centuries, from 1450 to the mid-1700s, Europeans described with accuracy, interest, curiosity, and insight the dress or habit, to use their term, of the Africans they met. The wealth of description offered by Olfert Dapper, first published in Dutch in 1668 and in French in 1686, was echoed and plagiarized by many later writers. For example, his descriptions were pirated by John Barbot, whose English text, published in 1732, became a major source of information for traders and explorers, and has been used in this essay.

What is most fascinating and useful in these and other reports is the basis they furnish for comparison with more recent costume, for recording constancy and change in fashion and in the techniques of manufacture of the textiles and jewelry of Africa.

COSTUME should serve to adorn the wearer, adding both material luster and a sense of well-being. This pleasure in adornment must be universal; it takes no effort to sense in the wearer of a beautiful necklace the glow of self-esteem conferred by such ornament.

Obviously, the elements of costume vary widely in different cultures: what is minimally acceptable dress in one may be little more than a bunch of leaves, a *cache-sexe,* or a penis cap (page 12), and in another it may be a complicated assemblage of garments. The individual's sense of propriety is not only defined but enforced by the parent culture. Ultimately, though a mode of dress may appear strange or even ridiculous to outsiders, only the values of the parent culture are of consequence or meaning for the wearer.

Indeed, each culture evolves its own distinctive fashion that serves to distinguish it from other groups. Thus the costumes of the Yoruba woman from Nigeria (page 13) and the Masai girl from Kenya (page 14) clearly express separate traditions. Both women, along with the Limam (page 18) of Larabanga Mosque in Ghana (once known as the Gold Coast) and the Kumu tribesman (page 15) from the Republic of Zaïre (formerly the Belgian Congo), exhibit the serene sense of self-assurance that results from knowledge of one's status combined with an awareness of occasion. The result: an unshakable sense of propriety, of secure self-esteem.

In Africa, as elsewhere, one can find superior taste demonstrated through either restraint or abundance. A minimal costume may carry for some groups the same prestige as an accumulative one does for others. In 1732 Barbot noted, with some astonishment, the spare dress of upper-class men on the Gold Coast who "wear only a fine clout about their waist, a cap made of fine deer's skin on their heads, and a staff in their hands, with a string of coral about their necks; by this their habit looking rather like poor than rich men: but I know not for what reason, they being as haughty as any other men in office."[1]

African attitudes toward the accouterments of rank seem to declare themselves in three views: first, prestige dress must be conspicuous. Second, it may announce itself with sound. Third, it is often additive. Thus, prestige may declare itself by a conspicuously visible and audible accumulation of ornament.

The third concept, that high dress is essentially additive, can be demonstrated in several examples. The Masai girl exhibits an obvious sense of wealth by addition; her accumulation of metal and bead necklaces is an instance of the whole equaling more than the sum of its parts. A similar abundance of clothing, paint,

(continued on page 16)

12

opposite above CACHE-SEXE. Mofu, Cameroon. w. 7 in. R. H. Lowie Museum of Anthropology, Berkeley, California. An element of women's dress, meeting Mofu society requirements of both modesty and fashion.

opposite below PENIS CAPS. Zulu, South Africa. L. 3⅜ in. The Peabody Museum of Salem, Massachusetts. Collected between 1905 and 1950. Demonstrate the concept of a critical minimum in male costume.

right YORUBA WOMAN dressed in high fashion for a Sango festival at Iseyin, Nigeria, 1968. The cloths, European in origin, are worn in traditional wraparound fashion.

above MASAI GIRL from Kenya. Wealth and prestige are reflected in her accumulation of finery.

opposite KUMU MAN, eastern Republic of Zaïre (formerly the Belgian Congo). His necklaces of leopards teeth and helmet of leopard hide are probably power symbols.

scarification, hairdressing, and jewelry is noticed in a number of early travelers' reports. For example, Thomas Astley described the wives of the King of Dahomey: "These women were rather loaded than adorned with Gold Necklaces, Pendants, and Bracelets, Foot-Chains of Gold and Silver, and the richest Jewels."[2] Individual pieces, such as the Yoruba necklace from Ife (page 16) also demonstrate this taste for adorned adornment; here the larger beads are graced with their own circlets of smaller ones.

Costume often carries its own sound, not only in the rustling of cloth but also in the accumulation of metal bangles that may ring, chime, or clank. Barbot recorded that Ivory Coast peoples loaded "their legs with vast thick iron rings. I have seen some . . . with above sixty pounds weight of such rings on one leg. They much admire the noise those rings make when they walk; and therefore the greater a man's quality is, the more rings he wears."[3] He also noted that brass bells were worn about their ankles and as armlets. "I saw some, who had iron rings about their legs, which weigh'd above three pounds each; but more of the bells, and other sounding ornaments, which please them at their publick festivals . . . and these they delight in, because they make a noise as they walk, and much more in dancing."[4]

Douglas Fraser has suggested that high fashion might be defined by the principle of opposites.[5] That is, the contrast between courtly and vulgar dress would lie mainly in the visible differences in the value or quantity of the materials. Such distinctions certainly exist in present-day Africa where prestige and fashion decree that only certain types of cloth or jewelry or costume are appropriate for certain occasions.

Usually, a sense of propriety, prestige, or prerogative has little to do with comfort. Rather, the self-assurance, the certain knowledge of one's own impeccable taste, sets aside as inconsequential minor or even major discomforts. Indeed discomfort may itself become the mark of prestige. Wearing anklets (page 17) causes an Ibo woman of high stature to waddle; but without them the woman still walks as if she had them on to declare her right to them and their attendant prestige. In 1700, the women in the region of the mouth of the Congo River were reported to have adorned "their Arms and Legs with bright Copper Rings and Armlets, several of which weigh ten Pounds Weight apiece, which makes them walk slowly, and in a Sort of affected Way."[6]

Adornment and costume affect the gestures and movements, similarly, of the modern-day Kamberi male dancers (page 22), who wear clanking iron anklets on one leg and use a stamping action in their choreography. At the same time their clothing is minimal and does not constrain or direct their movements.

opposite NECKLACE of glass beads. Yoruba, Nigeria. L. 10 in. Collection Dr. and Mrs. Roy Sieber, Bloomington, Indiana. Collected in Ife in 1971. An example of design through accumulation, each large bead having its own circlet of smaller beads.

right BRASS ANKLET. Ibo, Nigeria. D. 13½ in. University Museum, Philadelphia. Worn in pairs by women of high status. Their size causes inconvenience in walking, gladly borne because of the prestige they confer on the wearer.

LIMAM ("KEEPER") of Larabanga Mosque, Ghana, dressed in typical northern fashion, 1967. His gown, tailored from strip cloth woven on a man's horizontal loom, is a very old type of prestige costume.

Peggy Harper has suggested that wearing tight clothing or little clothing tends to result in actions and in dance movements that retain the energy of gesture within the torso. In contrast she notes that loose clothing which "requires continuous adjustment" results in "characteristic gestures of arms and hands, and adds to the tendency of throwing the body weight into their gestures. . . ."[7] (page 21, top). Long flowing robes would seem to encourage, if not require, broad, outwardly flowing gestures that cause a garment to balloon, flap, and swirl (page 21, bottom). Thus clothing which conditions everyday gestures may equally determine the character of dance.

References to adult nudity in Africa are fairly rare although certainly not unknown. An early-eighteenth-century report of peoples in the Cross River area bordering modern-day Nigeria and Cameroon stated: "They go quite naked, smearing their Bodies with a Sort of red Colour. They have several Scars on their Foreheads made with a red-hot Iron, or Pincers, plaiting their Hair in various Manners, and filing their Teeth as sharp as needles. . . ."[8]

Sudanic cattle-keeping peoples such as the Nuer and some agricultural groups in northern Nigeria, northern Ghana, and Upper Volta are among those for whom nudity, or near nudity, was reported a century or less ago. Yet, in most areas, some form of body covering was in general use, except among children. Until recently, Barbot's description of children on the Gold Coast would have applied nearly everywhere: "The youngest people of both sexes, about the coast, are seldom cloathed till eight or ten years of age, but go stark naked, playing, bathing, and swimming together, without any distinction. . . ."[9]

The achievement of adulthood is in part celebrated by the assumption of adult dress. Coming-of-age ceremonies (page 20) may include the change, symbolically, from nudity to dress. Ga girls in northern Ghana undergoing initiation into womanhood seem to enact this move over a period of several months. Yet, as children they are now rarely nude, and contemporary adult fashions are quite different from the garments associated with this ceremony. It appears to be one of a number of instances where older fashion survives principally or solely in ritual use. Another example occurs in the costumes of masked dancers and in woodcarvings depicting clothing or hair arrangements, these often the only traces of otherwise totally abandoned fashions of dress.

Ceremonial costume, however, need not involve survivals of past fashion, for often only the best of the new is selected for

(continued on page 23)

opposite GA GIRLS of Ghana in a coming-of-age ceremony, 1967. In this dance the girls wear beads and cloths in one stage of the passage from childhood nudity to adult dress. The change in fashion of adult women's dress is demonstrated by the contrast between the clothing of the ballet mistress and that of the women in the background.

above YORUBA WOMAN DANCING at Ipele, near Owo, Nigeria, 1969.

below YORUBA DEVOTEE of Sango-Egun dancing at a festival in Nigeria, 1968. The costumes of the dancers are used to accentuate the gestures of the dance.

KAMBERI DANCERS at Gebbi, Nigeria, 1969. Wearing heavy iron leg rattles, they use a stamping action in their dance. The weight and sound of the leg rattles in part determine the dancers' movements.

ritual use. For example, some costumes of the Yoruba *egungun* masquerades are concocted of the most fashionable of imported clothes. Furthermore, their impressiveness would seem to lie in part in the costliness of the cloths.

Because fashions do change, a brief survey of the descriptions of early travelers will give us an insight into those aspects of African costume that have disappeared and those that have persisted and have become national dress.

The Portuguese explorer Cado Mosto described the dress of the men on the Senegalese coast in 1455: "Their shirts reach to half their thighs, the sleeves of which are large, but cover only half of the arm. They use cotton drawers, which hang down to the small of the leg, and monstrously wide, being from 30 to 35 and forty palms in circumference; so that when tied on, they are full of plaits and though like a sack before, the hind part trails on the ground like a tail, resembling large petticoats with a train."[10]

A similar description appeared two centuries later in Dapper, and still later was copied by Barbot. Barbot's text makes it clear that Cado Mosto had given a description of the clothing of the nobles: "*The* APPAREL OF the prime men, is a sort of shirt, or frock of striped cotton of several colours; as yellow, blue, white, black &c. Some of these are plaited about the neck, others plain, having only a hole, or slit for the head to pass through, and reach from the neck to the knees with large open sleeves. Under this shirt they wear a thick cloth, made up after the fashion of long wide breeches, by them call'd *Jouba,* as is worn by the *Arabs,* much resembling a Woman's petticoat, plaited and tied around at the bottom; and is very inconvenient, as much obstructing the motion of the legs, because of the wideness and the thickness of the cloth it is made of. This sort of breeches is most used in the winter, for in the summer they wear only a single shirt of old linen, with a little cap made of leather, or ozier, streight at the head, but wide above like a large frier's hood."[11]

The plate from Dapper (page 25, top) illustrates this mode of dress. The man to the left wears a costume like that discussed. The umbrella, first described in about 1350 by Ibn Battuta for the court of the old Kingdom of Mali, is also an indication of his high status and is still associated with leadership and prestige in Ghana, Dahomey, and Nigeria. The family group to the right represents, in Barbot's term, "the common sort." The men wear a "short cotton clout" or a leather girdle.

An early English trader, Towerson, on a visit to what is now Liberia, recorded in 1555 that "people go all naked; except a clout to cover their nakedness, about a quarter of a yard long, made of the bark of trees, which will spin small, after the manner of linen. . . ."[12] This early English reference is useful because it describes ordinary dress, and because it indicates that woven bast or raffia cloth was in use, perhaps as a predecessor of cotton.

"Others again join several cloths or clouts, two or three fathom in length, which they wrap about their shoulders, and under the arms, and leave the two ends hanging before and behind down to their heels, like a long cloak, which they look upon as an honourable dress," wrote Barbot in 1732; women wore two cloths, one as a waistcloth and the other "over their heads in the nature of a veil."[13]

Sandals for the gentry, "trinkets of gold, coral or glass" worn in plaited hair arrangements by the women, and baubles and *grigri* for those who could afford them completed the costumes.

Later descriptions recapitulate the earlier reports in all essentials: tailored tunic and breeches were worn by the upper classes, and loincloth or wraparound skirt with cape or veil were worn by the commoners. However, the appearance of the tunic and breeches on the west coast seems limited to the Senegal-Gambia area until the late eighteenth century. Except for one reference to northerners called Malay (Mali?) at Whidah (Dahomey) dressed in "long, wide robes . . . which hang down to their heels with long broad sleeves [and] a large peeked cap fastened to the robe,"[14] so-called northern, or tailored, dress seems not to have been fashionable along the coast.

The basic garment on the coast from approximately modern-day Liberia east and south to Angola, was a loincloth or wraparound skirt and at times a cloak or mantle. This mode of dress, essentially the same for rich and poor except for the quality and amount of fabric used, was recorded in Barbot as worn along what is now the Ghana coast. "The common habit of the men consists of three or four ells, either of sattin, cloth, perpetuanas, sayes, *India* chints, or other sort of stuff; which without any help of taylors they throw about their body, roll it up in a small compass, and make it fast, so that it hangs from the navel downwards, covering all the legs half way. . . . When rich persons go about the town, or a visiting, they put on their best apparel, as has been mentioned above; or wrap about their necks and shoulders, two, three, or four ells of . . . richer stuffs . . . one end passing under their arms, like a cloak, holding a long rod, or javelin in one hand, with a grave mien, and follow'd by a slave, carrying a little low wooden stool."[15]

above COSTUME ON THE SENEGAL COAST, from Olfert Dapper, *Description de l'Afrique . . .* (1686, p. 234). The dress of a noble at the left is contrasted with that of a lower-class family to the right.

below COSTUME FROM LOANGO, from the 1686 edition of Dapper (p. 324). Most of the clothing here is made from woven raffia fiber: a long, fine, soft wraparound skirt is worn under a smaller, heavier cut-pile overskirt to which animal pelts are added.

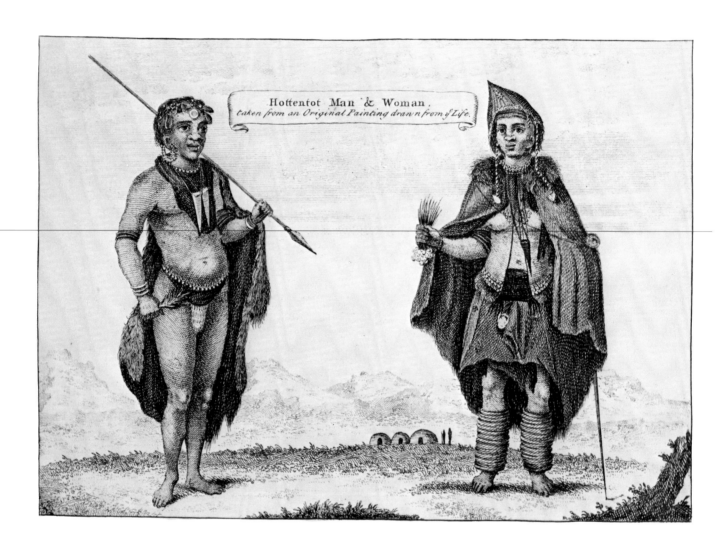

The dress of the women was much richer than that of the men. In addition to paying a great deal more attention to hair arrangements, cosmetics, scarification, rings, bangles, and necklaces, they wore cloths that were "two or three times as long and broad as [those] of the men. This long cloth they wrap around their waist, binding it on with a slip of red cloth . . . about half an ell broad, and two ells long, to make it fit close to the body. . . . The upper part of their body they cover with a veil of silk, or other fine stuff. . . ."[16]

Barbot, observing that all but a few women—chiefs' wives and possibly priestesses—"must attend housewifery, as the meanest slaves might do," was forced to conclude that "it appears, those females are not so lazy and haughty as some would represent them."[17] For those women who had to contribute to the work of the household, house dress consisted of a "country cloth," a term generally applied to locally woven cotton cloth that reached from waist to knees.

The dress of the Akreens, or Ga, of the eastern coast of modern Ghana was very similar. The men were described in the late eighteenth century as wearing a loincloth between their legs and looped over a leather or beaded belt. Fashion decreed that the back end hang lower than the front. The size—approximately ninety by twenty-three inches—seems closely related to that of modern cloths woven by women on upright looms.[18]

Larger cloths, about three yards square, served as blankets at night, lounging dress in the morning, and wraparounds during the day. To serve as a lounging dress, the cloth was wrapped around the body so that one arm was left uncovered. Later in the day, it was considered improper *not* to leave the upper half of the body bare; therefore the cloth was then wrapped around the waist and the end tucked under the belt on the left side. This sort of man's garment would seem to resemble mantles or togas such as *kente* cloths, which are worn today by the Akan men of Ghana and are made from narrow strips woven by men on horizontal looms. These large cloths would not stay securely tucked and were easily loosened with movement or in excitement. Thus they constantly needed adjustment; fastening and loosening became a pastime that reminded one traveler of the game European ladies played with a fan.

The Akreen women's dress was similar: a loincloth, supported by a rather narrower belt, and a large cloth worn as a wraparound. A second large cloth, finer than the skirt, was worn as a shawl. Children went nude until the age of eight; after that and until marriage, only one large cloth was worn, leaving the upper part of the body bare.

Essentially the same sort of dress was worn eastward along the Slave Coast—modern Togo, Dahomey and Nigeria, as far, at least, as Benin. However, status demanded in some instances that five or six rich cloths be worn one on top the other but always with the upper torso left bare.[19] The result, visible in Benin plaques and modern ritual dress at Benin, is a tendency for the male figure to become bell-like in silhouette. Other aspects of ceremonial dress at Benin need serious study, for some seem derived from European and particularly Portuguese prototypes, military or ecclesiastical.[20]

Another illustration from Dapper (page 25, bottom) depicts the costume of the area near the mouth of the Congo River. Again, the wraparound skirt was the basic costume. Perhaps the most significant historical aspect of the dress of this area was that locally made, finely woven raffia long remained in fashion. An underskirt, reaching from waist to ankles, was of fine, almost gauzelike raffia; the smaller overskirt, also of woven raffia, was embroidered to resemble velvets. Finally, animal skins were worn on top of the overskirt.

An early traveler observes "a surprising Art in making various Sorts of Cloths, as Velvet, cut and uncut, Cloth of Tissue, Sattins, Taffeta, Damasks, Sercenets, and such like" from palm-tree fibers: this description of raffia, or "palm-tree-cloth," comes from Lopez, whose reports were published about the middle of the sixteenth century and quoted later by Astley.[21] Early records also occasionally indicate that raffia cloth was made in Liberia and Dahomey, and with more frequency report it from the Gabon and the Congo.

Thus, from Senegal to Angola there existed a basic mode of dress: an untailored wraparound skirt or loincloth and a mantle or shawl. Worn by both men and women, it was made of cotton or raffia, with cotton predominating in the western stretches of the coast and almost totally absent in the southeast.

Princely or prestige dress was clearly of two types: a tailored, "Turkish" or "Moorish" fashion of tunic and breeches, described in early reports from the area of Senegal and Gambia, and an elaborated version of the basic costume, found along the remainder of the coast. In the mid-1600s both fashions seem to have been found in the area of modern Liberia.

From Angola south to the Cape, and possibly along at least a portion of the east African coast, costume was made of leather rather than woven fibers. But again the breechclout or the skirt and cape seem to have been the essential units of dress. The following description of Hottentot dress (page 26) from the area of modern South Africa is based on a voyage made in 1705:

"Their *Krosses,* as they term them, or the mantles they hang over their shoulders, are worn open or closed according to the season. The krosses of the most wealthy are of tyger or wild cat-skins; and those of the common people of sheep-skins: in winter they turn the hairy side inwards, and in summer turn it outwards. They lie upon them in the night, and when they die, they are tied up and interred in them. . . .

"The women wear caps all the year round, made of the skins of wild beasts, that point up spirally from the crown of the head. They generally wear two krosses round their shoulders, which, like those of the men, cover their backs, and sometimes reach down to their hams. Between these krosses they fasten a sucking child, if they have one, with the head just peeping over their shoulders."[22] The observer goes on to report that bullrush rings are worn on the lower legs by girls until about the age of twelve, when the rings are "laid aside, and their place is supplied with rings of the thickness of a little finger made of slips of sheep or calf-skins, from which the hair is singed; for the *Hottentot* sheep have nothing like wool. Some of the women have above an hundred of these rings upon each leg so curiously joined, and so nicely fitted to the leg, and to each other, that they seem like curious pieces of turnery. They are smooth and as hard as wood, and make a clattering noise in dancing. These rings are kept from slipping over their heels by wrappers of leather or rushes about their ankles; and as the women are obliged every day to walk through bushes and brambles to gather roots and other things for food, they preserve their legs from being torn by the thorns and briers. These rings are one great distinction of their sex, and are considered as very ornamental; for the more rings they wear, the finer they are reckoned: but this is not all, they are provisions against an hour of hunger and great scarcity; for when that arrives, they pull them off and eat them."[23]

In much of Africa there are obvious parallels between modern dress and the descriptions in early reports. Tunics and breeches almost exactly fitting the early descriptions are widespread but seem primarily an inland fashion; thus, in Sierra Leone (page 30), Liberia (pages 31, 39), and Nigeria (pages 32–38), they are more frequently found upcountry than on the coast. Bowdich, on a visit to the inland city of Kumasi (in modern-day Ghana) in 1817, was "surprised by the sight of the Moors" wearing "large cloaks of white satin, richly trimmed with spangled embroidery, their shirts and trowsers were of silk, . . ." and their turbans were of white muslin.[24] Quite possibly this type of dress appeared along the west coast as a costume of prestige rather recently. One example of this sort of dress is a suit from Dahomey

(continued on page 40)

MAN'S ROBE. Sierra Leone. L. 48 in. The American Museum of Natural History, New York. A robe in brown with black warp stripes, further decorated with stamped black circles. Similar in style to that described nearly three hundred years ago as prestige costume from Senegal to Sierra Leone.

MAN'S GOWN. Liberia. W. 70 in. The Museum of
the Philadelphia Civic Center. Similar to a prestige robe, also decorated with figurative embroidery, illustrated in George Schwab, *Tribes of
the Liberian Hinterland* (1947, Fig. 77b). That
gown was owned by a Mano chief and considered an heirloom of northern origin.

BOY'S COSTUME. Yoruba, Nigeria. Tunic: 40 x
28 in. Collection Donald M. Thieme, Nashville,
Tennessee. Collected in 1965. Tailored costume,
with tunic, drawstring breeches, and hat. The
style of the embroidery differs from that of the
Hausa (also of Nigeria) but resembles that of
groups in Dahomey.

MAN'S ROBE. Hausa, Nigeria. W. 100½ in. The
Museum of Primitive Art, New York. Collected
in 1964. A *riga,* a large loose robe with elaborate embroidery departing from the usual
Hausa motifs (see page 38). The *riga* is worn
bunched at the shoulders. Eyelet embroidery of
natural colored local silk covers the central
panels, back and front.

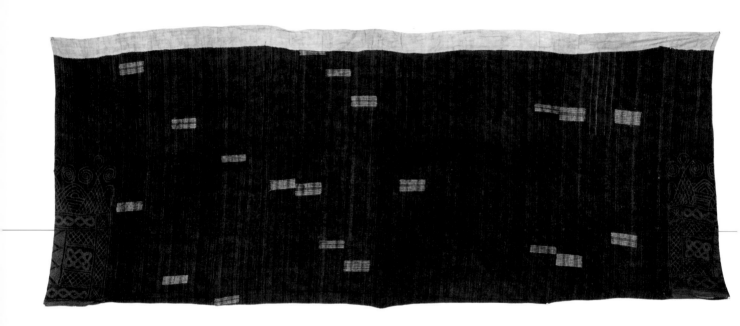

above DRAWSTRING BREECHES. Hausa, Nigeria. w. 20 ft. The American Museum of Natural History, New York. Francis Moore, in *Travels into the Inland Parts of Africa,* 1738, reports that he saw breeches seven yards wide which the men of the Gambia River area wore gathered around their middles. The embroidery of this example (green on a blue-and-red-striped cloth) is typical of modern-day northern Nigeria.

opposite DRAWSTRING BREECHES. Yoruba, Oyo, Nigeria. w. 48 in. The American Museum of Natural History, New York. Collected in 1951.

DRAWSTRING BREECHES (*detail opposite*). Hausa, Nigeria. w. 81 in. Field Museum of Natural History, Chicago. Collected in 1929 by W. D. Hambly. The embroidery of typical Hausa patterns appears to be in the colorful style of Kano.

above MAN'S ROBE. Hausa, Kano, Nigeria. W. 100 in. The American Museum of Natural History, New York. Collected in 1948. A *riga* with typical Hausa embroidery designs. The extent of the embroidered area reflects the wealth of the owner.

opposite MAN'S ROBE. Liberia. L. 48 in. Collection Mr. and Mrs. Jo Dendel, Costa Mesa, California. Six different stripe patterns, including one tie dye, edge-sewn to produce a single tunic.

(page 41). This costume of embroidered tunic and breeches is said to have belonged to Behanzin, King of Dahomey from 1889 to 1894. A shark, the traditional symbol of Behanzin, is appliquéd on the breeches and would seem to support that attribution. The tunic, however, closely resembles one in the Musée de l'Homme, Paris, that is simply designated as a warrior's shirt.[25]

The use of untailored garments—wraparound skirts and mantles—worn by both men and women, still continues in much of West Africa. For example, Yoruba women (pages 13, 21) wear skirts, shawls, and head-cloths of untailored rectangles of cloth either locally made or imported. *Kente* (pages 198, 199), now a national costume in Ghana, is the traditional mantle or toga of the early descriptions. Both locally produced cloths and imported European cloths are worn in the same fashion.

Examples of special types of dress are masquerade costumes used in religious rituals. These are rarely mentioned in the early literature, but have been extensively recorded in recent times. They include net costumes and tightly fitted suits, knitted or appliquéd (pages 42—44), and are often accompanied by masks. These costumes, however, are not the proper object of study in this essay, for the emphasis here is on garments that enhance rather than hide the wearer's identity.

Another form of special dress is found in the apparel of hunters and warriors. The addition of protective charms and power symbols lends a surreal quality to essentially normal garments. The nineteenth-century war dress from Senegal (page 45) is a cloak magically made impregnable through the addition of incantations in Arabic script and leather-encased charms called *grigris*. Similarly, the Maninka hunter's tunic and the Dan-Ngere example are covered with protective charms—teeth, claws, and horns, which are symbols of power (pages 46, 48, 49).

The garment used as a war tunic in southern Ghana (page 47) is quite unlike the usual togalike dress of the Akans, and would seem to have a northerly origin. Called the *batakari,* it is found as ordinary dress in northern Ghana (page 50); when covered with amulets and power symbols, it becomes a magically invulnerable uniform of war. Bowdich illustrated an Ashanti war captain who appears to be wearing a *grigri*-covered tunic (page 51).

Barbot, in a long passage described the *grigri* of West Africa: "Whatsoever was the original of these *Grigri*,... people will willingly part with any thing they have to be furnish'd with as many as they are able to purchase, according to their quality and profession; and take a great pride in them. Some will give two or three slaves for one *Grigri*; others two, three, or four oxen, answerable to the virtues or qualities assign'd to it. I was told,

(continued on page 53)

ROYAL COSTUME. Fon, Dahomey. Tunic: L. 35 in. The Brooklyn Museum, New York. A sleeveless tunic, trousers, and hat decorated with appliqué and embroidery. Possibly the costume of Behanzin, King of Dahomey in the late nineteenth century, whose symbol was the shark (see fish motif on the trousers). The bull's head on the cap may symbolize the sun.

42

opposite APPLIQUED COSTUME. Ibo, Nigeria. L. 66 in. Field Museum of Natural History, Chicago. Collected in 1966 by Herbert M. Cole. Many well-known types of Ibo masks, such as Maw, require the wearing of tightly fitted, complex, appliquéd costumes of this sort.

above CHILD'S KNITTED COSTUME. Senufo, Ivory Coast. 36 in. Collection Anita J. Glaze, Champaign, Illinois. Collected in 1969. Basic costume of the boys who are to be initiated in Poro, a men's society. Its wear constitutes the first ritual step leading ultimately to adulthood. The belt cut from an automobile tire has iron bells attached.

above DANCE COSTUME. Liberia. L. 17 in. Milwaukee Public Museum. Collected in 1926. Probably used in Poro bush school. The garment is of knotted netting with a cut-pile edging encircling neck, waist, and sleeves.

opposite WAR DRESS. Senegal. L. 39 in. The Museum of the Philadelphia Civic Center. Collected in 1889. The Arabic script and leather amulets were probably meant to make the wearer invulnerable in battle.

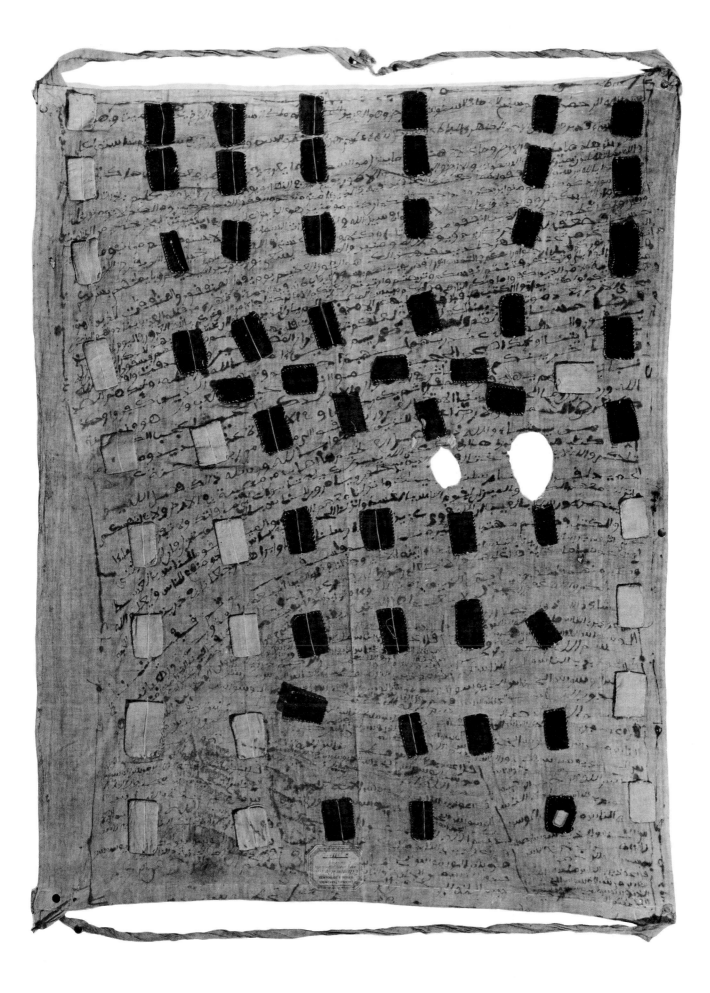

HUNTER'S DRESS. Maninka, Korhogo, Ivory Coast. L. 33 in. Collection Charles and Joan Bird, Bloomington, Indiana. A tunic covered with power symbols, such as horns, claws, and teeth.

WAR DRESS. Akan, Ghana. L. 30 in. UCLA Museum of Cultural History, Los Angeles. A northern type of smock, the *batakari,* covered with amulets containing words from the Koran, as well as other charms worn to safeguard a warrior and to insure his success in war.

HUNTER'S DRESS (*back view opposite*). Dan-Ngere, Ivory Coast. L. 30 in. Private collection. A tunic laden with bundles of medicine and horns, expressing the ritual power of the hunter.

above TUNIC. Dagomba, Tamale, Ghana. L. 35
in. Collection Dr. and Mrs. René A. Bravmann,
Seattle. A *batakari* or *fuugu,* a popular north-
ern-Ghanaian men's garment (see page 47). It
is tailored from strips of local cloth woven by
men on a narrow horizontal loom.

opposite ASHANTI WAR CAPTAIN wearing a
war tunic. From a drawing made in 1817 by
Thomas E. Bowdich, leader of the first official
British visit to Kumasi, and published in 1819
in *Mission from Cape Coast Castle to Ashantee.*

opposite left WAIST ORNAMENT. Jaba (Ham), Nigeria. D. 9 in. Collection Dr. and Mrs. Roy Sieber, Bloomington, Indiana. Collected in 1958. A woman's waist or buttocks ornament, meant to insure her modesty when she bends over to work in the fields. The outer rim is decorated with imported beads.

opposite right BELT AND WAIST ORNAMENT. Nkundo, Mongo, Republic of Zaïre. L. 30 in. UCLA Museum of Cultural History, Los Angeles. Gift of the Wellcome trust. A woman's belt of plaited and twined raffia, worn low on the hips. The cut-pile pom-pom, worn at the back, bobbles provocatively as the wearer walks.

that *Conde*, . . . [the] viceroy, . . . constantly wore to the value of fifty slaves in these *Grigri's* about his body; and so every other person of note proportionally: for not only their caps and waistcoats, but their very horses are covered with them in the army, to prevent being wounded. To say the truth, some of the principal *Blacks* are so well furnish'd all over with *Grigri's* in every part of their bodies, under their shirts and bonnets, that they cannot well be wounded with any *Assagaia,* or javelin; nay, they often stand in need of being help'd to mount their horses, which are also adorn'd with the same, to render them more sprightly, and prevent their being hurt."[26]

Protective charms, still in use in Africa, are usually bits of paper covered with sentences from the Koran and folded and encased in cloth or leather. Each has its particular meaning and use: ". . . some to prevent being cast away, when they go a fishing; some to save them from being wounded, killed, or made slaves in war, or as they travel; others to secure them against thunderbolts; others to preserve women in child-bed; others to excel in swimming, to get many wives, or much wealth, to have a good fishery, and to all other purposes which relate to their welfare. In short, they have as much confidence in them, as ignorant people place in relicks, and therefore will boldly expose themselves to any danger."[27]

A large number of costume elements are difficult to classify. Some may be worn around the waist, for example, but really do not qualify as loincloths or wraparounds. The "waist cloth" with a cut-pile pom-pon (page 52, right) is worn rather low over the buttocks and bounces provocatively as the woman walks. A Jaba waist ornament (page 52, left) is also worn at the back, but it serves as a modesty protector when the woman bends over. The Lumbwa and Tswana examples (pages 54–56) are called aprons, a somewhat confusing term, for it is often unclear whether they are to be worn at the front or back, as underskirt or overskirt. The feather cape (page 57) was presumably worn over the shoulders, but the uses of other garments (pages 58–60) are not so easy to determine. These might have been capes for men or women, wraparound skirts for women, or back skirts—long draped cloths extending from waist to heels but open at the front to display a small beaded apron.

Not at all difficult to classify and among the most wildly and wonderfully inventive elements of African dress are hats (pages 62ff). Early descriptions indicate the fascination with which Europeans viewed the variety of unexpected forms of headgear they encountered. One account tells of ". . . a long osier [basketry] cap, like a *Mitre*, beset with a few goats horns, porcupine

(continued on page 61)

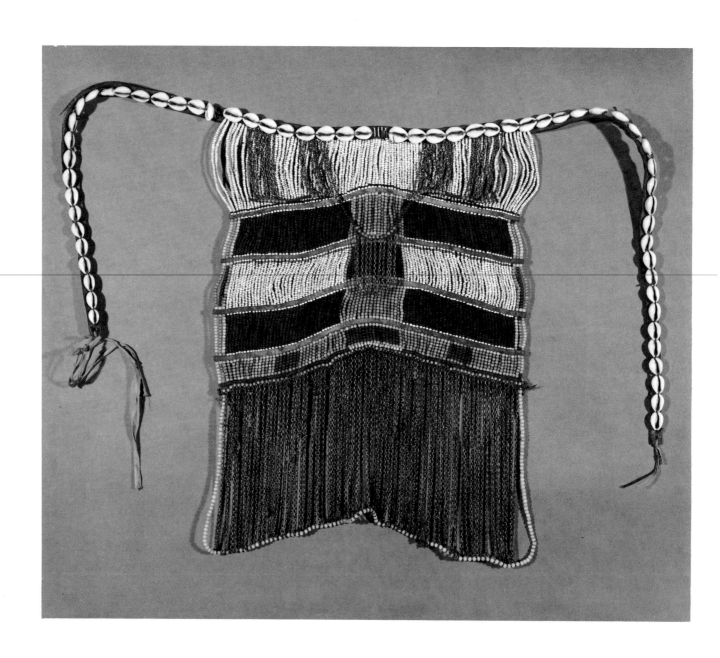

above WOMAN'S APRON. Lumbwa, Kenya. L. 18 in. The American Museum of Natural History, New York. Collected in 1949. A ceremonial skirt consisting of a leather and cowrie belt to which strands of imported beads and chains are attached.

opposite WOMAN'S APRON. Tswana or Sotho, Botswana. L. 14 in. University Museum, Philadelphia. Collected before 1912. Leather and beaded waist ornaments, or aprons (see page 56), are worn by women of several groups in southeastern and southern Africa.

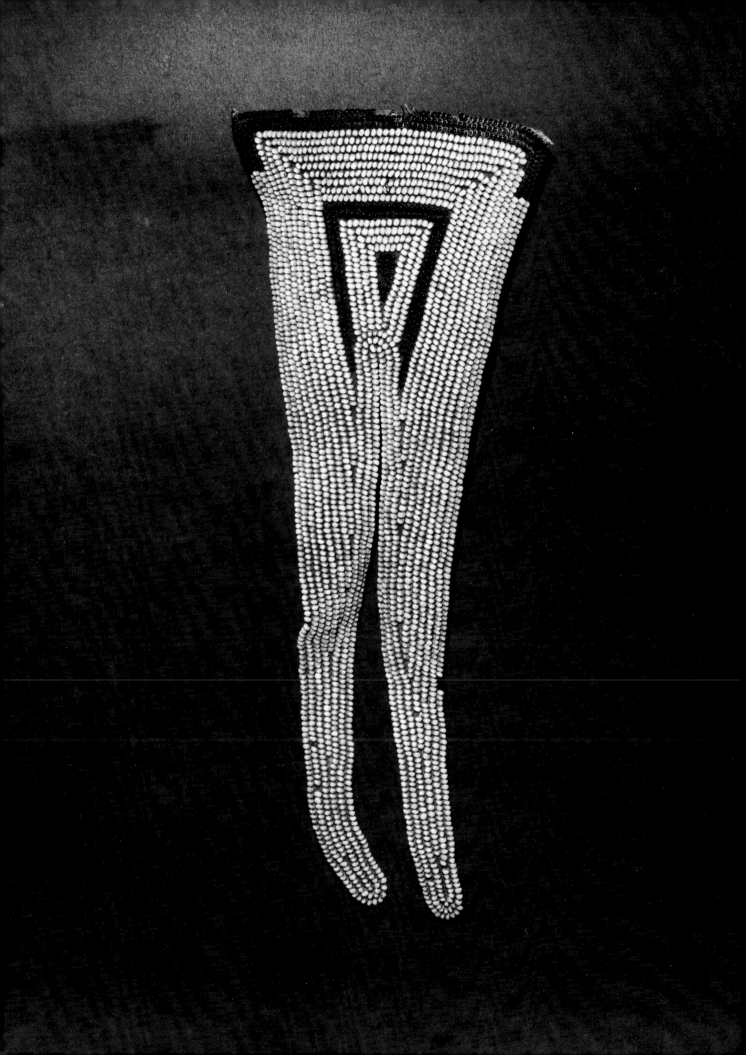

above WOMAN'S APRON. Tswana or Sotho, Botswana. L. 26 in. Private collection.

opposite FEATHER CLOAK. Cameroon. L. 44 in. Collection Katherine White Reswick, Los Angeles. A cloak resembling costumes covered with feathers and like them, probably used ritually.

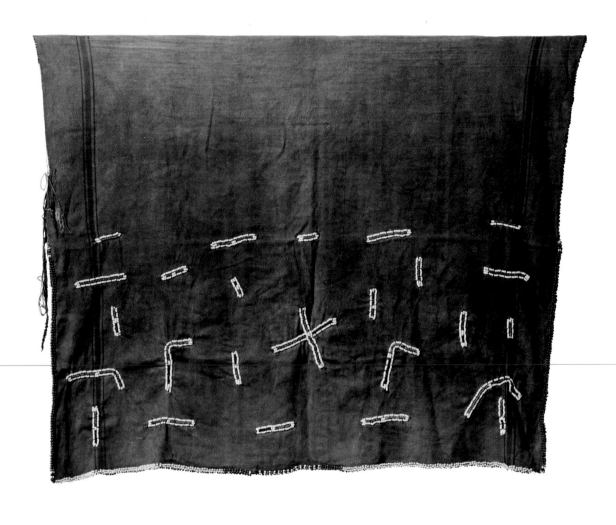

above SKIRT OR CAPE. Nguni (?), South Africa. w. 38 in. Buffalo Museum of Science. Collected about 1900.

opposite SKIRT OR CAPE. Nguni (?), South Africa. w. 43 in. Buffalo Museum of Science. Collected about 1900. European cloth decorated with imported beads. Cloths of similar size and decoration, worn as capes or skirts, are known to have come from the Pondo and Xosa, subgroups of the Nguni.

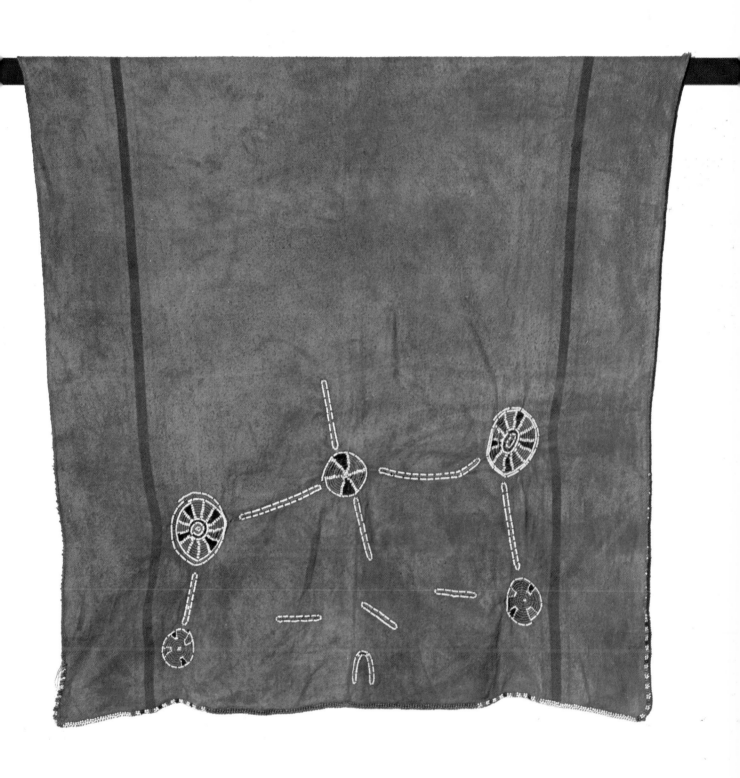

CAPE OR SKIRT. Origin uncertain. w. 47 in. Museum of African Art, Washington, D.C. Leather cape (or backskirt) with beaded decoration. Comparable leather garments are found among a number of groups ranging from the Masai of Kenya through the Sotho to the Hlubi (Zulu) of South Africa.

tails, and *grigris*."[28] To hats of rushes or goat or dog skins were added "some small goat's horns, gold toys, and little strings of the bark of their consecrated tree, and some add monkey's tails to all the rest."[29] The latter may be a chief's hat because of the reference to gold toys. The goat horns (more probably duiker horns) are symbols of power and strength.

Barbot described war helmets, apparently of the Akan: "The officers...wear caps made of the skins of elephants, or buffaloes, in the nature of helmets, garnished with the jawbones of men, killed by them in battle. Others adorn them with red and white shells, goats-horns, and idols. Others again have caps made in the shape of morions, of lions, tygers, or crocodile's skins, covered all over with ears of *Indian* wheat, cocks-legs, feathers, monkeys skulls, and other charms."[30]

The King of Whidah (Dahomey) "was dressed in the most magnificent Manner, and had on his Head a gilt Helmet, with white and red Feathers."[31] And from the coast of the Congo comes a reference to "a kind of Hats made of the Barks of Trees, or Nut-Shells."[32]

Hats are concocted of a variety of materials ranging from a base of leather and cloth to calabash and basketry, decorated with cowrie shells, horns, beads, seeds, feathers, and *grigris*. They are sewn, stitched, plaited, woven, crocheted, and appliquéd. The results range from a reasonably ordinary hat to a Yoruba king's crown (pages 65, 62). According to Yoruba legend, the creator God, Oduduwa, initiated the use of such beaded crowns. He sent sixteen of his sons out from the center of the world, Ile-Ife, to establish the basic Yoruba kingdoms; each was granted the right to wear a beaded crown and only their successors may now wear them. The veil of beads at the front of the crown protects the king's subjects from the danger of staring at his face. The bird at the top would seem to be a symbol of the king's communication with the gods and the spirits of departed kings.[33]

Somewhat less exalted levels of authority are represented by the Cameroon chiefs' or elders' hats (pages 64, top; 68–70), the Kuba hat of blue and white beads (page 64, bottom left, and the Pende chief's horned crown of beads (page 71).

Two of the hats relate to war. The Liberian basketry hat (page 72) is now the badge of a champion bush cutter, but once it may have been a champion warrior's helmet.[34] The *grigri*-covered cloth cap (page 73) from Ga territory in eastern Ghana is described in a letter of 1890: "... the fetish cap formerly belonged to a Captain of a company ... and was worn by him in a war

(continued on page 80)

opposite BEADED CROWN. Yoruba, Nigeria. H. 36½ in. The Brooklyn Museum, New York. King's crown, related to the myth of origin of the Yoruba. Each of the kingdoms expresses its origin and its association with the creator god, Oduduwa, by means of a beaded crown.

right MUNGA BOWMAN in northern Nigeria in service of Sheikh of Bornou; detail of engraving, based on a sketch by Major Dixon Denham, in his *Narrative of Travels and Discoveries*... (1826, opp. p. 166).

below SENUFO MAN wearing a plumed basketry hat reserved for a champion cultivator, rewarding his endurance, strength, and skill. ca. 1970.

opposite above HAT. Cameroon. D. 36 in. Private collection. Collected by Dr. Paul Gebauer (a Baptist missionary in the Cameroon). A chief's hat of feathers. When the mesh cap is turned inside out, the hat collapses into an easily stored bundle of feathers.

opposite below left BEADED HAT. Kuba, Republic of Zaïre. H. 9½ in. The College Museum, Hampton Institute, Hampton, Virginia. Collected by William H. Sheppard ca. 1900. A prestige hat of cowries and imported blue and white beads and bells over a basketry foundation.

opposite below right HAT. Gola (?), Liberia. D. 17 in. National Museum of Natural History, The Smithsonian Institution, Washington, D.C. Collected in 1874. A spectacular example af additive decorations over a basic hat type.

right HAT. Senegal. D. 14½ in. The Museum of the Philadelphia Civic Center. The coiled basketry hat of the western Sudan ranges from a flattened cone to a clearly demarcated rim and crown, as in this example.

above FEATHER ORNAMENT. Kuba, Republic of Zaïre. H. 4 in. National Museum of Natural History, The Smithsonian Institution, Washington, D.C. Collected in 1899. Possibly a prestige hat.

opposite KIKUYU MAN from Uganda, far from the Cameroon Grasslands (see page 64 top), demonstrates the widespread use of feathers as head decoration. 1914.

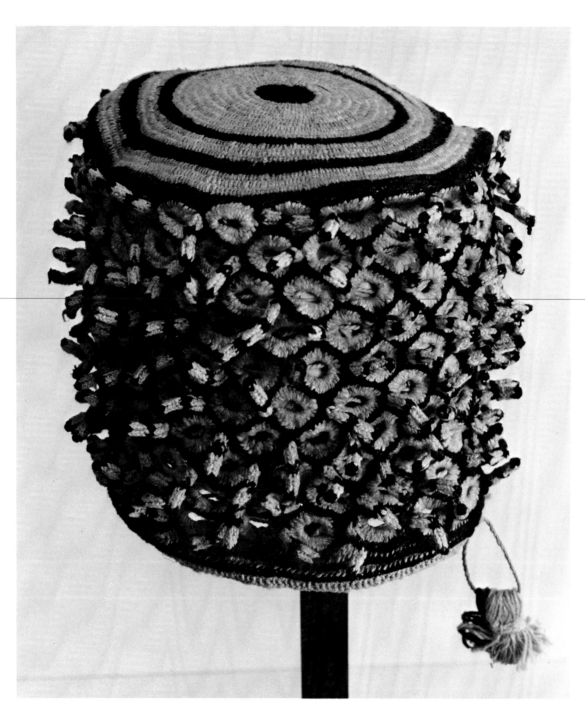

above HAT. Cameroon. H. 6½ in. Private collection. Collected by Dr. Paul Gebauer.

opposite HAT. Tikar, Cameroon. H. 16 in. Private collection. Collected in 1934 in Ngambe by Dr. Paul Gebauer. A chief's hat of cotton and feathers, a type often depicted in Cameroon sculpture.

opposite HAT. Cameroon. H. ca. 14 in. Private collection. Collected by Dr. Paul Gebauer. A chief's hat of appliquéd cotton cloth. The technique is also used on tunics and robes.

above BEADED HAT. Pende, Republic of Zaïre. W. 16 in. Collection Dr. Daniel P. Biebuyck, Newark, Delaware. Collected in 1954. A western-Pende chief's hat. Blue, white, and yellow beads are attached to a fiber framework.

above COILED BASKETRY HAT. Liberia. D. at bottom 9 in. Peabody Museum, Harvard University, Cambridge, Massachusetts. Collected in 1927. A champion bush cutter's basketry helmet.

opposite WAR HAT. Ga, Ghana. H. 16 in. The Peabody Museum of Salem, Massachusetts. Collected in 1889. A warrior chief's hat covered with protective charms.

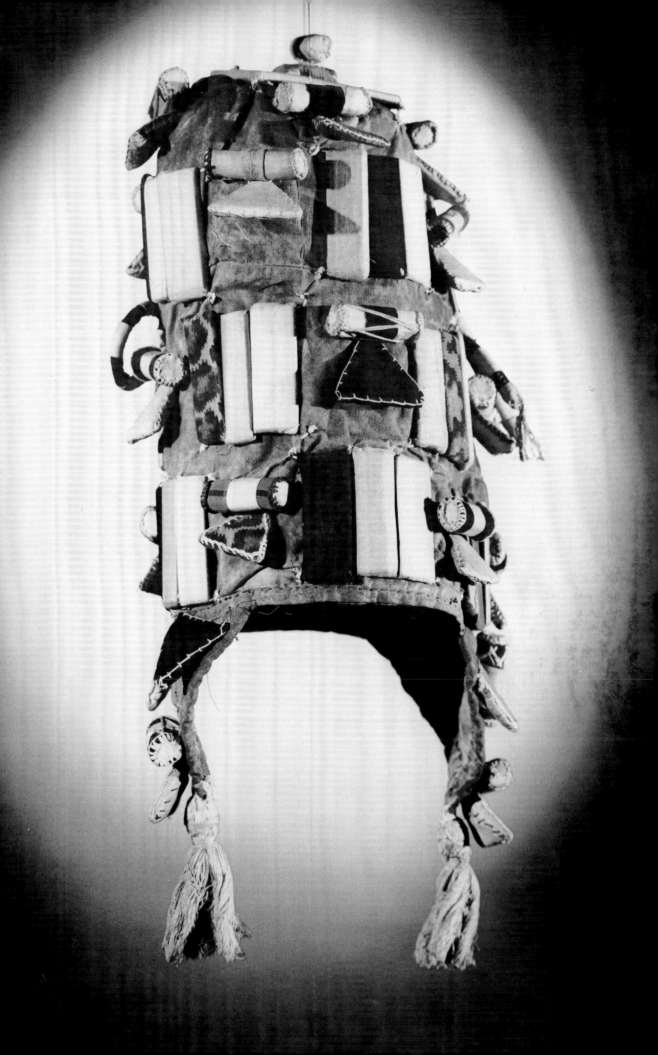

HAT. Gola, Liberia. D. 15 in. The Museum of the Philadelphia Civic Center. A conical hat of leather and cut-pile raffia.

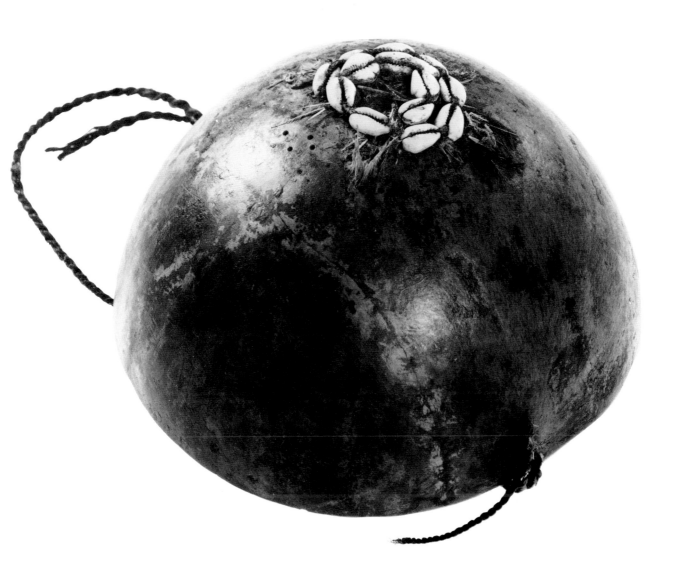

HAT. Bargu, Togo. D. 7½ in. National Museum of Natural History, The Smithsonian Institution, Washington, D.C. A calabash helmet decorated with cowries and feathers, possibly a war helmet.

75

above HELMET. Nigeria. H. 15 in. Collection
Dr. and Mrs. Roy Sieber, Bloomington, Indiana.
A basketry helmet covered with abrus seeds,
probably from the area of Pankshin.

opposite DANCE CAP. Bemba, Republic of
Zaïre. H. 16 in. The Museum of Primitive Art,
New York. Gift of Mr. and Mrs. John J. Klej-
man. A cap of twined basketry covered with
cowrie shells topped by the tusk of a forest pig.

opposite HAT. Lega, Republic of Zaïre. H. 10½ in. UCLA Museum of Cultural History, Los Angeles. A head ornament of feathers, fiber, and cowrie shells.

above HAT. N'gola, Angola. H. 10 in. University Museum, Philadelphia. Collected before 1927. A chief's hat of raffia fiber.

which occurred in February 1888. The captain was afterwards hung for murder during the war."[35]

Shoes, when worn, were usually simple sandals of fiber or a piece of leather tied on with thongs. More elaborate, highly decorated sandals (page 84, top) are still part of the regalia of leadership. Wooden clogs (page 84, bottom), reflecting the influence of the Arab world, are known in several parts of east Africa.

Riding boots (page 85) of appliquéd leather may be associated with the western Sudan. The horse, introduced from the north, brought with it an array of trappings. These were often decorated with appliqué and embroidery on leather. In nineteenth-century illustrations, horsemen wear decorated riding boots, and their horses are adorned with saddle cloths and chest and face plates, most of which were probably of appliquéd leather. So-called "morocco leather" may have originated south of the Sahara. All the plants used in the treatment of the leather as well as those used to dye it (including the millet plant whose stalk yields the characteristic rusty-red color) are to be found in the stretch of West Africa where leather is cured and dyed today.[36] Appliqué and embroidery may have developed in emulation of Near Eastern prototypes, but the results now are typically and recognizably West African.

Many African costumes would be considered incomplete without the inclusion of some device such as a whisk, weapon, or fan as an insignia of rank or prestige (page 87).

The carrying of a whisk to brush away insects is a prerogative of elders in many parts of Africa. Although goat- or cow-tail switches are the most common, one seventeenth-century report described "a small whip, the handle of black wood, and loaded with ornaments, the cord of the whip being of silk. . . ."[37] Probably the most spectacular example in American collections, and possibly outside of Africa, is an elephant-tail whisk from the Ashanti (page 86). It was taken from the palace of the Asantehene, or ruler, in Kumasi during the British punitive expedition on February 5, 1874.[38] Bowdich, who visited Kumasi in 1817, saw the Asantehene during a ceremony where "elephants tails, waving like a small cloud before him, were spangled with gold. . . ."[39]

Swords and other weapons frequently figured in ritual as symbols of the might of leadership. In ceremonies a sword may have been carried by the ruler, for example, or borne before him as an emblem of his strength and military prowess. It may also have been used by a subordinate, who, dancing and gesticulating with the weapon, declared his allegiance and submission to the leader.

(continued on page 89)

FAN. Benin, Nigeria. L. 23 in. Field Museum of Natural History, Chicago. Gift of Mrs. A. W. Fuller. Fans are carried by chiefs and nobles in Benin and used to cool the Oba (king) during rituals. This example was collected by Ralph Locke, one of the two survivors of the massacre of January 4, 1897, that led to the Benin Punitive Expedition later the same year. Most of the major Benin bronzes were brought out as prizes of war during that campaign.

above SCARIFICATION patterns on a young married woman of the Kingdom of Gulagu, Mandara Mountains, Nigeria.

opposite SCARIFICATION patterns on a Senufo woman from Pundya village, Ivory Coast. Hers are coming-of-age scars.

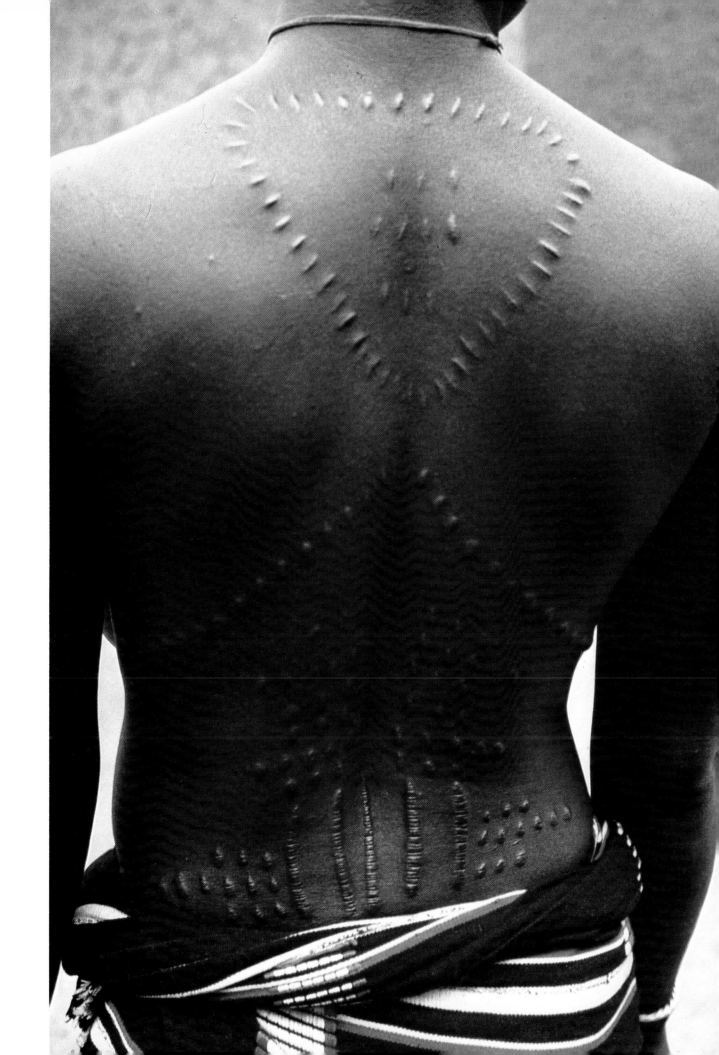

above SANDALS. Hausa, Kano, Nigeria. L. 12½ in. The Herskovits Collection, Evanston, Illinois. Prestige sandals of leather and ostrich feathers presented to the late Melville J. Herskovits by the Emir of Kano in 1931. They were an exact copy of sandals worn by the Emir.

below WOODEN SANDALS. Rhodesia. L. 10 in. Royal Ontario Museum, Toronto, Ontario. Moslem-style sandals of the type known in east Africa, probably introduced as a result of trade across the Indian Ocean. These show evidence of long wear.

opposite BOOTS. Origin unknown. L. 45 in. UCLA Museum of Cultural History, Los Angeles. Gift of the Wellcome trust. Riding boots, probably from northern Nigeria, of so-called "morocco leather" with appliqued designs. This technique is known from North Africa southward through the western Sudan into the northern forest region from Ghana to Nigeria.

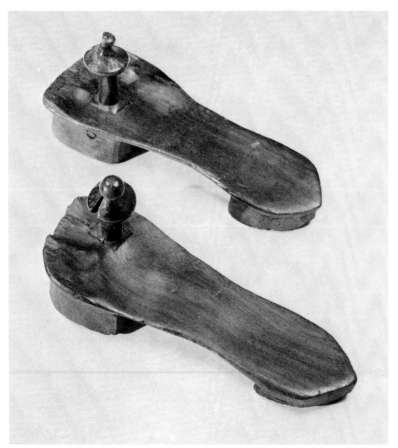

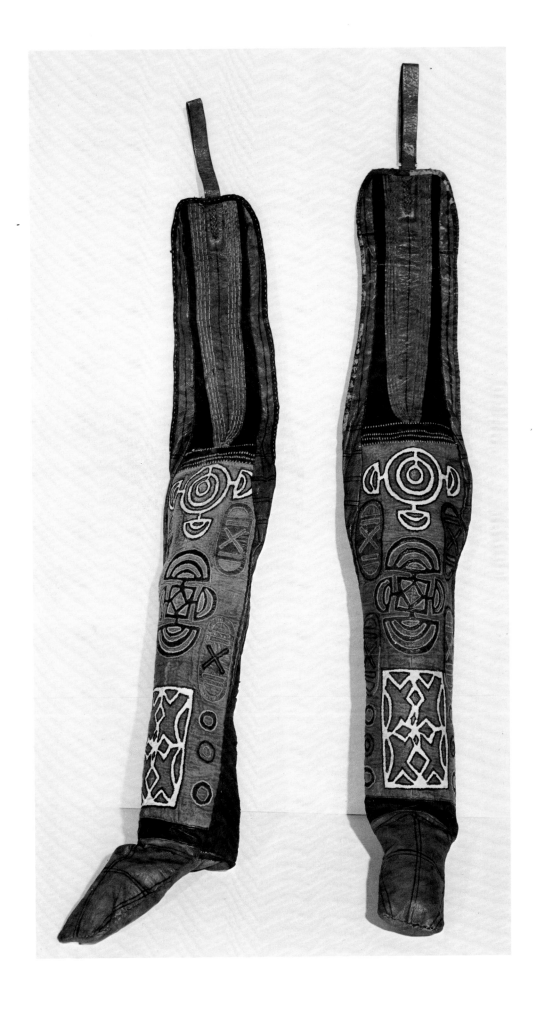

opposite WHISK. Akan/Ashanti, Ghana. L. 20 in. UCLA Museum of Cultural History, Los Angeles. Gift of the Wellcome trust. Collected in 1874 in Kumasi by Capt. J. E. Audley Harvey of the Black Watch. Made of an elephant's tail, the handle covered with embossed sheet gold fastened with gold studs and plaited strips of gold and silver. Some of the hairs have beads of glass, coral, or bone strung on them. The beads were probably more valuable than gold.

right MUNZA, King of the Mangbetu, sitting in full dress on his throne, holding a falchion as a symbol of power. After a sketch by Georg Schweinfurth, in *The Heart of Africa,* 1874 (vol. 2, frontispiece).

88

The Kuba knife (page 88) is an exceptional example of a royal sword. It was presented to William H. Sheppard, the first missionary to the Kuba and the first Black missionary in the Congo, by the son of the king. Its use is described by Sheppard:

"The king or Lukenga, as he was called, sat high in a pavilion with his family and chiefs around him. The master of ceremonies laid the long knife before the chief of each tribe in turn. The chief picked it up and stepping out into the circle faced the king, saluting with the knife. Then he dances as the big drums beat and the long ivory horns blew. After this he made his speech about the progress of his people."[40]

The leaders may also be protected with umbrellas or cooled with fans. The prince of Ardra, who displayed "an Air of Grandeur and Dignity, tempered with a Sweetness, that at once gained him Love and Respect," was attended by "two Officers [who] constantly fanned the Prince with Fans of Scenthed Leather."[41] The Prince of Popo "has many handsome Women, two of whom stand always by him, with Fans in their Hands, to cool him."[42] Leather-appliqué fans (page 81) are used today in a similar manner at Benin. During ceremonies, the Oba, or king, is cooled with long hard strokes of the fan, not with flutterings. Fans from more northern areas are often edged with ostrich plumes (page 88).

BODY DECORATION of the African fascinated the early European travelers, who often remarked on the handsomeness of the groups they encountered. Before discussing the costume, cosmetics, and other ornaments of the peoples of the central Guinea Coast, Barbot noted:

"The *Blacks*, in this part of *Guinea*, are generally well limb'd and proportioned, being neither of the highest nor of the lowest size and stature; they have good oval faces, sparkling eyes, small ears, and their eyebrows lofty and thick. Their mouths not too large; curious clean, white and well-ranged teeth, fresh red lips. ... For the most part they have long curled hair, sometimes reaching down to their shoulders ... and very little beards before they are thirty years of age. The elderly men wear their beards pretty long. They are commonly broad-shoulder'd, and have large arms, thick hands, long fingers, as are their nails, and hooked small bellies, long legs, broad large feet, with long toes; strong waists, and very little hair about their bodies. Their skin, tho' but indifferent black, is always sleek and smooth. . . . In short, they are for the most part well-set, handsome men in outward appearance. . . .

opposite left FAN. Igbira, Nigeria. L. 27 in. UCLA Museum of Cultural History, Los Angeles. Gift of the Wellcome trust. Collected before 1936. A northern type of fan decorated with ostrich feathers.

opposite right CEREMONIAL KNIFE. Kuba, Republic of Zaïre. L. 29 in. The College Museum, Hampton Institute, Hampton, Virginia. A forged-iron sword that once belonged to Lukenga, a king of the Kuba. Presented by Lukenga's son to William H. Sheppard, who described it as a symbol of royal authority.

"The *Black* women, I also observed to be strait, and of a moderate stature, pretty plump, having small round heads, sparkling eyes, for the most part, high noses, somewhat hooked, long curling hair, little mouths, very fine well-set white teeth, full necks, and handsome breasts. They are very sharp and witty; very talkative . . . very covetous, . . . and proud to a high degree; which is inferred from their costly dress, as if women in any part of the world, did not clothe themselves according to their ability."[43]

The natural beauty of the African was then and is today enhanced through a variety of means, and these fall into two categories: permanent alterations and temporary decorations. Permanent alteration results from scarification, or cicatrization; tattooing; cranial deformation; chipping, filing, or knocking out teeth; and piercing and stretching of lips, nose, and ears. Temporary decoration is accomplished with paint, powder, or irritant herbs, and in a fantastic variety of hair arrangements.

The designs achieved through scarification have been effected in two ways. If the healing process of small incisions is artificially retarded, the resulting scars form raised knobs, darker than the surrounding skin. If tiny, generally circular portions of skin are removed, the resultant scar is a small, circular depression usually lighter than the surrounding skin.[44] These scars on black skin become satinlike depressions or dark raised dots or lines; the effect is not only that of a subtle contrast of light and dark, but also a textural and, indeed, sculptural quality of black on black (pages 82, 83, 91). Along with acknowledging the beauty of scarification patterns, one must recognize the discomfort of acquiring them. Just as the "effort to be dressed up must involve expense and trouble" so scarification "is paid for in pain."[45] The person who has undergone scarification is rewarded by the knowledge that others not only admire the results but recognize the cost involved.

In the middle of the fifteenth century, Cado Mosto described patterns "which seem like Flowers on Silk wrought on Handkerchiefs, and never wear off."[46] In 1554 Captain John Lock likened the scars to flowered damask[47]; a year later Towerson suggested that the skin is "raised with divers works, in the manner of a leather jerkin."[48] The initiation of girls as priestesses as noted in Astley consisted of learning songs and dances, "and then they mark them, which is done by cutting their Bodies with some Iron Points, in the Form of Flowers, Animals, and especially Serpents. . . . Their Skin, after this, appears like a fine black, flowered Sattin, which has a pretty Look. . . ."[49]

Barbot recorded scarification in several places along the coast; typical is this description from the Gold Coast:

SCARIFICATION patterns on a Bwaka man from the Republic of Zaïre.

90

"Often making small incisions on each side of their faces, and sometimes imprinting figures of flowers, on their faces, shoulders, arms, breasts, bellies and thighs, with such art, that at a distance it looks as if their bodies were carved, for those figures rise above the rest of the skin, like a half-relief which I have observed in the women of Sestro and some men adorn their faces and arms in the same manner, it all being done with hot irons."[50]

Curiously, the scars were often described in early reports as if they resulted from burning, although that is unlikely. Some may have occurred this way, but more often burning was used medicinally and not to produce cosmetic scarring.[51]

Cicatrization, as the process is also called, may be a device for marking or identifying a family or a people. It may also be part of the process of initiation, symbolizing the move to adulthood or membership in a society or cult. Finally, it may designate status, in which case the growing accumulation of scars indicates the achievement of increasingly higher rank.[52] The permanency of the role or status is reflected in the permanency of the scars, for neither is reversible. In addition to any other significance they might have, the marks are intrinsically decorative, and are frequently considered intensely sensual. Scarification is, then, a complex, at times subtle, language communicating symbolic, aesthetic, and sensual meanings.[53]

PAINTED DESIGNS on a young female Yakoma dancer from the Ubangi River area, Republic of Zaïre.

Another mode of permanent modification of the body is the process of piercing—particularly the ear lobes, nasal septum, and lips—in order to hang, attach, or insert a decorative object. Ears are pierced for the insertion of earrings (page 99), or the holes stretched to insert ear plugs (page 103). These ear decorations are made of materials as precious as gold (pages 106, bottom; 101) and as common as pieces of straw or wood (page 103, bottom). Nose ornaments depend from a pierced septum (pages 104, 105), and labrets are fitted into pierced and stretched holes in one—or both—lips (page 100). Barbot describes the process as it was observed in the eighteenth century:

"A peculiar, but strange fancy in this people, is, to bore their upper lip, and thrust into it a small ivory pin, from the nose down to the mouth: others split their under-lip so wide, as to thrust the tongue through on ceremonial occasions. Most men and women, instead of ear-rings wear long silver rings of three or four ounces a-piece; others in lieu thereof, have pieces of a flat thin wood, as broad as the hand; or goats horns or ivory rings."[54]

Painting on face or body is another language that has been imperfectly recorded (page 92). Whereas scarification may reflect permanent change of status, paint may be used to symbolize more transient states. Cole notes that when the body paint used during public dances by Dan initiates is washed off, the girls "are proclaimed women and are then ready for marriage."[55] Red powders such as ocher, but especially camwood (*tukula*), are widely used as a cosmetic. Early travelers recorded their use as well: "*Tokkola* [is] a red Colour drawn from a certain wood ground on a Stone and mixed with Water, with which they daily paint themselves from the Waist upwards, thinking it a great Beauty."[56]

Barbot described the painting of face and body for what appear to have been special occasions: "They adorn their skin in most parts of the body, and just round one of their eyes, with scars in many fantastical figures, which they paint with a stuff composed of several ingredients, soak'd in the juice of a sort of wood called *Tocoel*; and observe nicely to paint a white circle round one eye, and a yellow one about the other, daubing their faces on each side with two or three long streaks of the same colours, each streak different from the other."[57]

Barbot further noted that dancers, priests and priestesses, and votaries and celebrants were often painted as a necessary part of ritual. Soldiers were painted to awe the enemy: "Their bodies are all over smear'd with yellow, white, red and grey colours, laid on like flames or crosses, very hideous to behold. . . ."[58] Today one may observe that priests in Ghana and warriors in Zaïre are similarly painted on ceremonial occasions.

Various cosmetic appurtenances, such as boxes for storing *tukula* and containers for mixing it (pages 95, 96), are common—as are mirrors, adopted and adapted from Europe, and at times set in elegantly carved holders (page 97).

Perfumes of civet and fragrant woods are used. Bits of fragrant wood are also at times made into necklaces. Tobacco, though not a cosmetic, gave rise to objects of personal use: pipes, tobacco pouches, and, especially noteworthy, delicate bottles of calabash or horn to carry snuff (pages 98, 102).

Cado Mosto admired the complicated coiffures of the Africans. "Both sexes . . . weave their hair into beautiful tresses, which they tie in various knots, though it be very short."[59] Other accounts refer to a fantastic range of hair treatment: "platted or twisted, and adorn'd with some few trinkets of gold, coral, or glass"[60]; a "coif, standing up five or six inches above their head, which they think a fine fashion"[61]; "They are very proud of their Hair; some wear it in Tufts and Bunches, and others cut it in Crosses quite over their Heads. . . . Others will let their Hair

COSMETIC BOX. Kuba, Republic of Zaïre. H. 7½ in. Collection Mr. and Mrs. Ernst Anspach, New York. A container for *tukula* (powdered camwood), which, when mixed with water or oil, serves as a cosmetic. The designs on the outside of the box and lid are like those embroidered on cut-pile raffia cloths.

(continued on page 107)

94

above MAKE-UP KIT. Kuba (?), Republic of Zaïre. L. 11¼ in. Collection Mrs. Judith Nash, New York. Probably used for moistening *tukula* (camwood) before application.

opposite MIRROR CASE. Ibo, Nigeria. L. 11¼ in. Collection Mr. and Mrs. Herbert M. Cole, Santa Barbara, California. Collected near Nsukka. Decorated with motifs similar to those of nearby Awka.

left SNUFF BOTTLE. Zulu (?), South Africa. H.
1¼ in. Buffalo Museum of Science. Collected
about 1900. Made of a small gourd with a sewn
pattern of brass and copper wire.

opposite FULANI WOMEN of Mali wearing gold
earrings and ornaments of amber.

left LABRET. Karamojong, Uganda. L. 1⅜ in. R. H. Lowie Museum of Anthropology, Berkeley, California. Collected in 1966. Aluminum plug worn through a hole in the lower lip.

opposite GOLD EARRINGS. Fulani, Mali. L. 6 in. Private collection. Among many peoples, personal wealth consists of jewelry—both for display and for safekeeping.

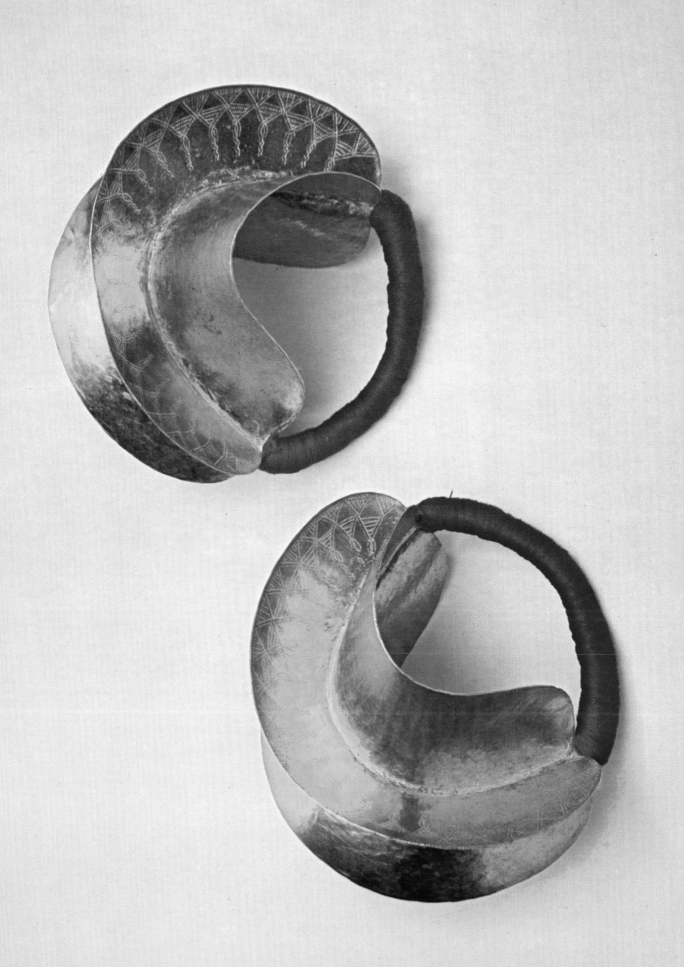

left SNUFF BOTTLE. Swazi, South Africa. H. 3 in. University Museum, Philadelphia. Collected before 1912. Made of carved horn and has a wooden stopper.

opposite above WOODEN EAR PLUG. Barabaik, Tanzania. L. 3½ in. The American Museum of Natural History, New York. Collected in 1954. Holes in ear lobes are stretched to carry large plugs of wood or ivory.

opposite below EAR PLUGS. Kanuri, Nigeria. Collection Dr. and Mrs. Arnold Rubin, West Los Angeles. Soft wood cylinders decorated with European paints: red, green, and yellow.

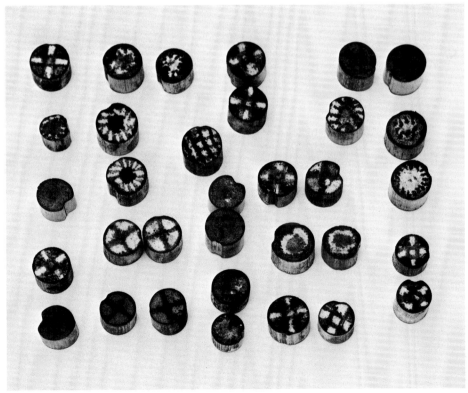

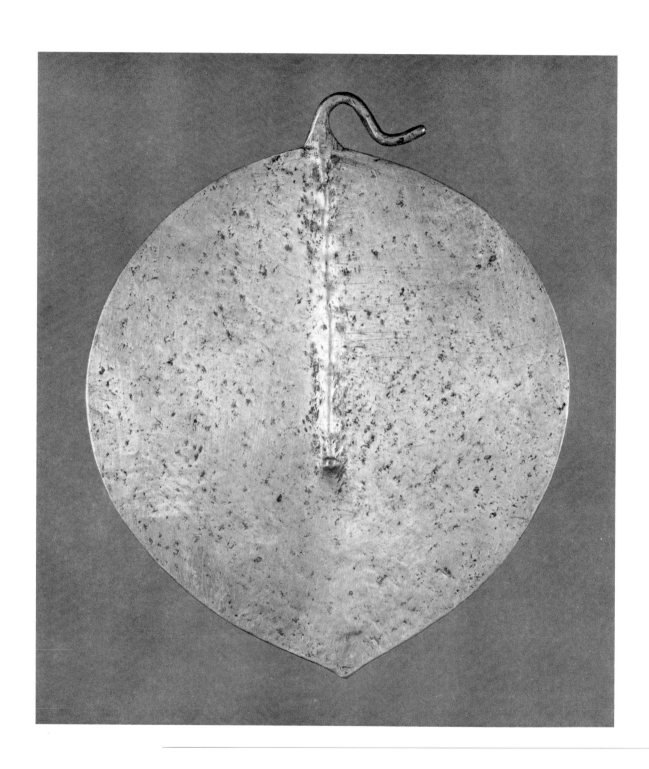

NOSE ORNAMENT. Turkana, Kenya. L. 5 in. The American Museum of Natural History, New York. Collected in 1948.

NOSE ORNAMENT. Karamojong, Uganda. L. 5¼ in. R. H. Lowie Museum of Anthropology, Berkeley, California. Collected in 1947/48. This ornament and the one opposite, of beaten aluminum, are from neighboring groups. They are worn over the lips, hanging from a pierced nasal septum.

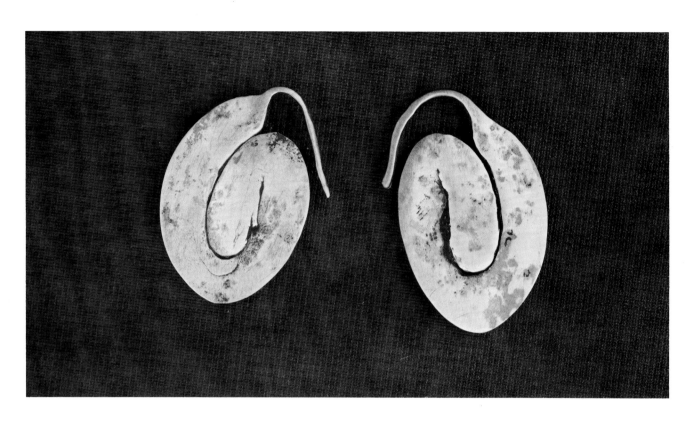

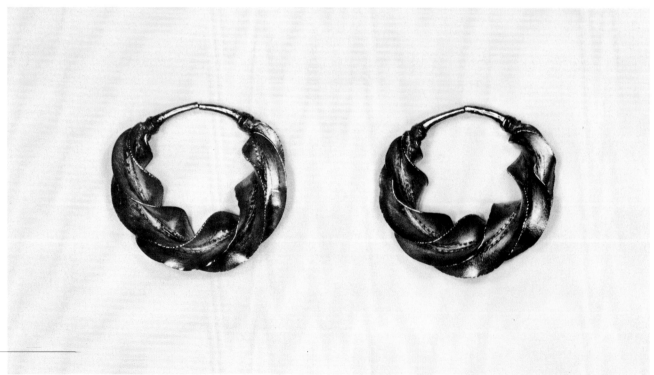

hang down on each Side of their Heads, plaited . . . on which they string Coral, and for want of it Pipe-beads. . . ."[62]

One of the most complicated arrangements was observed in Benin around 1700 by Nyendael: "They often content themselves with letting their Hair grow in its natural Form, except buckling [crimping] it in two or three Places, in order to hang a great Coral at it. But the Womens Hair is very artificially curled-up in great and small Buckles, and divided on the Crown, like a Cock's Comb inverted, by which Means the small Curls lie in exact Order. Some divide their Hair into twenty or more Curls, as it happens to be thick or thin; others oil it with Palm Oil: By this Means its black Colour turns, in Time, to a Sort of Green or Yellow, which they are very fond of. . . ."[63]

Nyendael also notes that in time of mourning, the wives, slaves, and nearest relations of the deceased shave all or part of their heads. Thus fashion and custom decree a wide range of hair arrangements—from shaved heads, which may mark the esteemed status of an Mbeere elder of Kenya, to extremely complex coiffures (pages 108–111). Often, fiber frameworks or gum or clay additives are used to control the form or to add body to the arrangement.

Wigs are used both for cosmetic and for ritual purposes. In the *Bwami* ritual of the Lega people, a female head-dress is worn by men of high status (page 108). Elsewhere, some masks, again usually worn by men, represent women with elaborate hair constructions; in such instances, the hair arrangement is either reconstructed or depicted with meticulous accuracy.

Complex hair arrangements will last for weeks or months; neck rests (or pillows) are used to support the head during sleep to avoid damaging the hair sculpture.

Body hair is often considered ugly or indecent and is shaved or plucked. African cosmetic kits frequently contain a variety of razors and tweezers, as well as combs of wood, ivory, or metal (pages 112–118, 121).

Whether artfully arranged or worn simply, the hair may also support or carry ornaments. As noted, small beads may be threaded into plaits, but also larger baubles of metal (page 120) or amber (page 99) may be used. Bead-covered ornaments tied at the side of the head are worn by Tutsi princesses (page 126). Some razors, pointed at one end, are worn as hair- or hatpins (page 122). Pins of bone, ivory, rattan, iron, or copper are worn by both men and women as decoration, as a means of securing hats, and, in the case of complicated coiffures, as scalp scratchers (pages 119, 124–126). Pins of these sorts seem much more common in the east and south than in western Africa.

(continued on page 123)

left above FULANI WOMAN from the western Sudan with elaborate coiffure. Her earrings are gold, the large beads at the back of her head and on her necklace are yellow amber. From *The Secret Museum of Mankind* (New York: Manhattan House, no date).

left below HAT in form of a wig. Lega, Republic of Zaïre. L. 12 in. Collection Dr. Daniel P. Biebuyck, Newark, Delaware. Collected in 1951. A hat made in imitation of woman's hair style by initiates of *Kindi*, the highest grade of *Bwami*, the men's secret society. The polished mussel shell represents the crescent moon.

opposite MANGBETU WOMAN from the Republic of Zaïre, her hair styled in the form of a flared cylinder. She wears two bone hairpins.

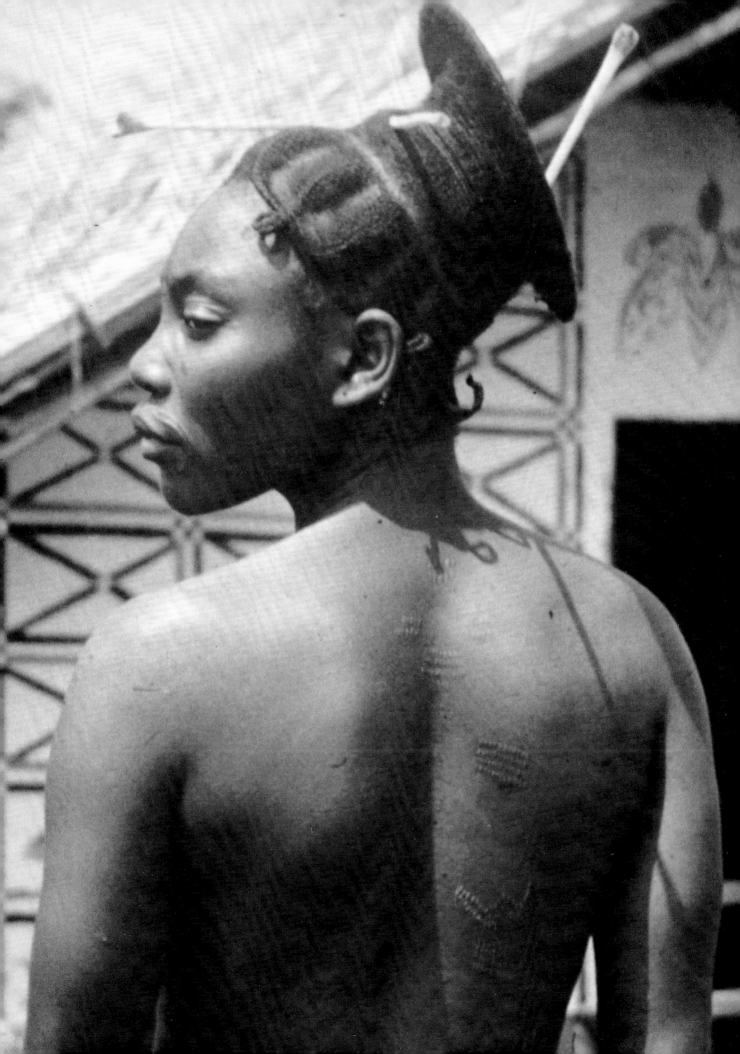

SHILLUK MAN whose hair arrangement is built
up of mud. From *The Secret Museum of Mankind* (New York: Manhattan House, no date).

IBO WOMAN of Nigeria with coiled hair and center crest. From *The Secret Museum of Mankind* (New York: Manhattan House, no date).

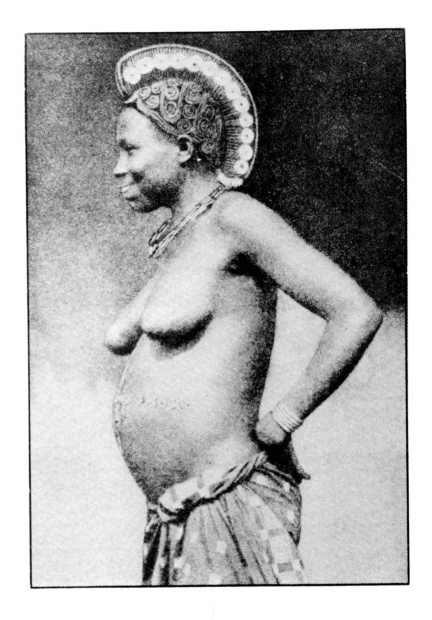

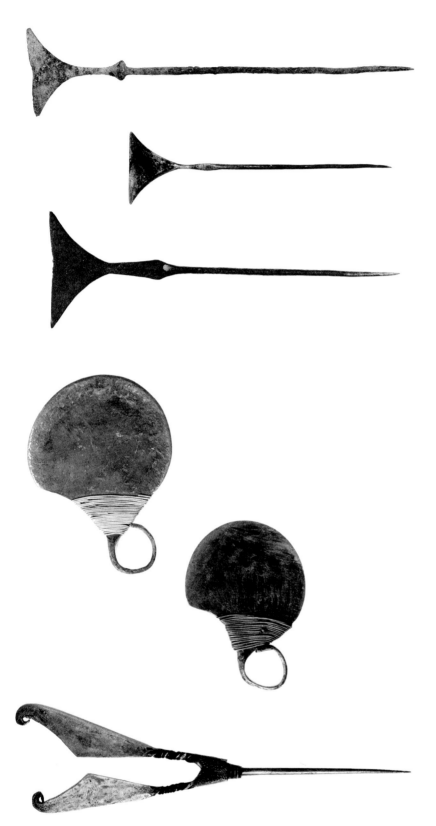

left above RAZOR PINS. Luba, Republic of Zaïre. L. 8⅜ in. UCLA Museum of Cultural History, Los Angeles. Used as hair ornaments, razors, and occasionally tools for scarification. A Luba woman without one or more razors in her hair would not be considered completely dressed.

left center FINGER KNIVES. Karamojong, Uganda. L. 4½ in. R. H. Lowie Museum of Anthropology, Berkeley, California. Collected in 1966. Worn as rings, these knives may have been used both as weapons and as razors by several groups in Uganda and Kenya, including the Karamojong and Suk.

left below RAZOR PIN. Angola. L. 8⅝ in. Royal Ontario Museum, Toronto, Ontario. An unusual double-bladed razor pin.

opposite SWEAT SCRAPERS/RAZORS. Lozi, Zambia. L. 4½ in. The American Museum of Natural History, New York. Collected in 1907 and 1915. Often called sweat scrapers, these spatulate iron tools also served as razors.

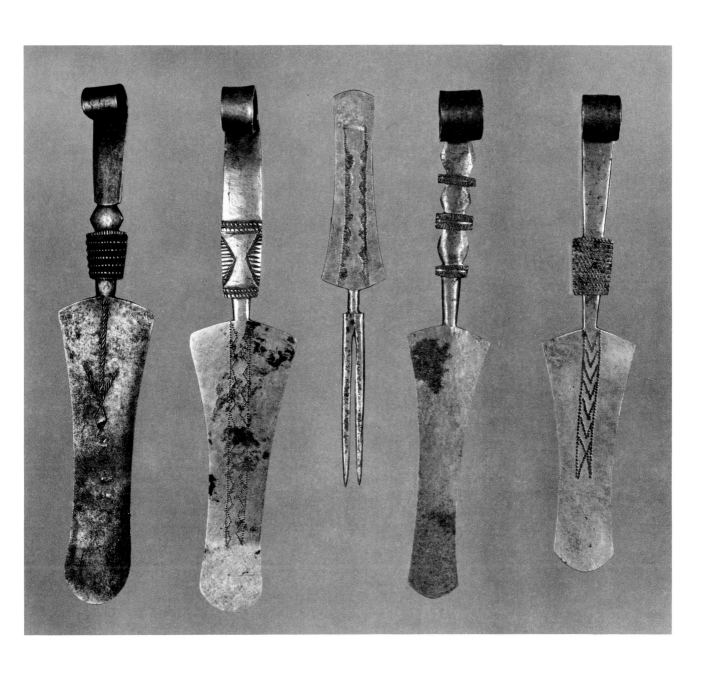

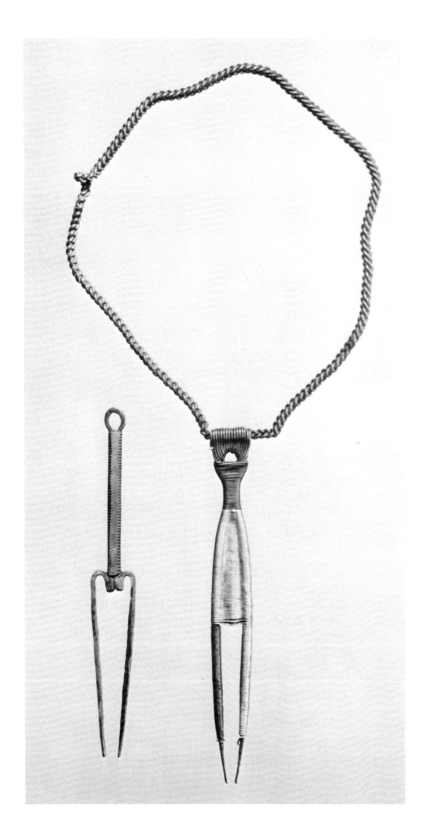

left TWEEZERS. Kamba, Kenya. L. 8⅛ in. University Museum, Philadelphia. Body and, at times, facial hair may be considered ugly or even obscene. It is temporarily removed by shaving, more permanently by plucking it out with tweezers.

opposite left IVORY OR BONE COMB. Republic of Zaïre (?). L. 6½ in. UCLA Museum of Cultural History, Los Angeles. Gift of the Wellcome trust.

opposite right WOODEN COMB. Akan, Ghana. L. 7½ in. Collection Mr. and Mrs. Ernst Anspach, New York. Thomas Astley reported in 1745 that combs, worn as ornaments on the Gold Coast, were used in one form of salutation by removing and replacing the comb with the left hand, "a Sign of great Respect among them."

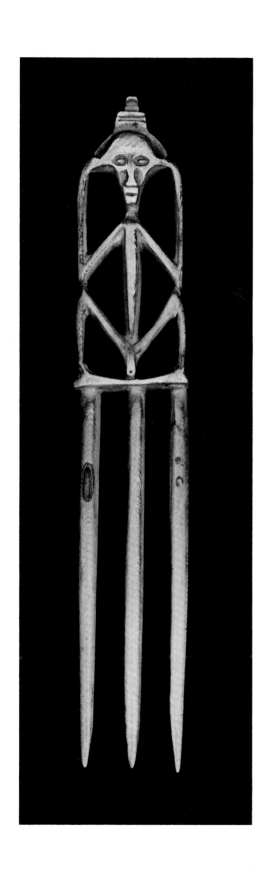

COPPER COMB. Kuba, Republic of Zaïre. L. 8¼
in. The College Museum, Hampton Institute,
Hampton, Virginia. This comb, originally having four teeth, was collected by William H.
Sheppard about 1900. It had belonged to the
Kuba King, Lukenga, and was said to be more
than a century old. It was worn horizontally,
so that beads (now missing) would fall forward
over the forehead and eyes.

WOODEN COMB. Uganda. L. 10 in. The American Museum of Natural History, New York.
Collected in 1946. A fan-shaped comb made by
lashing splints in place.

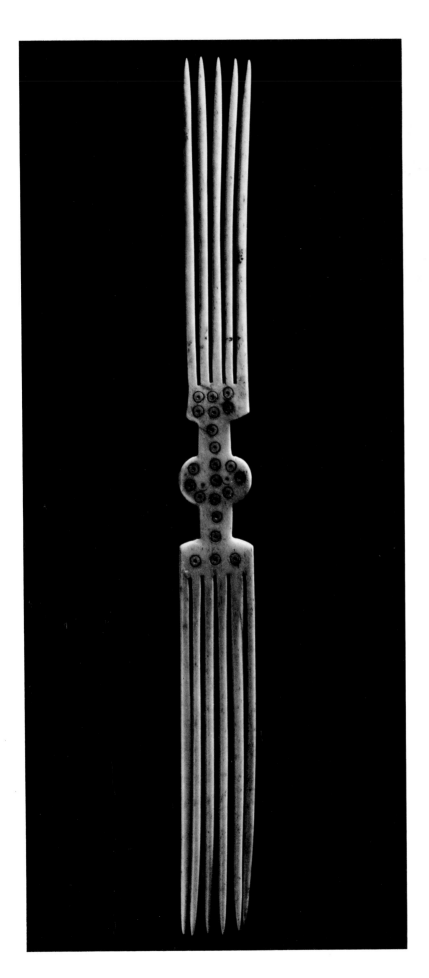

left BONE COMB. Zulu, South Africa. L. 9½ in.
Peabody Museum, Harvard University, Cambridge, Massachusetts. Collected before 1905.

opposite above HAIRPINS. South Africa. L. 12½ in. The American Museum of Natural History, New York. Bone and bead hairpins, possibly from the Zulu.

opposite below BRASS PENDANT. Bobo, Upper Volta. W. 3⅞ in. Private collection. The crescent shape may derive from a bird form; the projecting bird head closely resembles some Bobo masks.

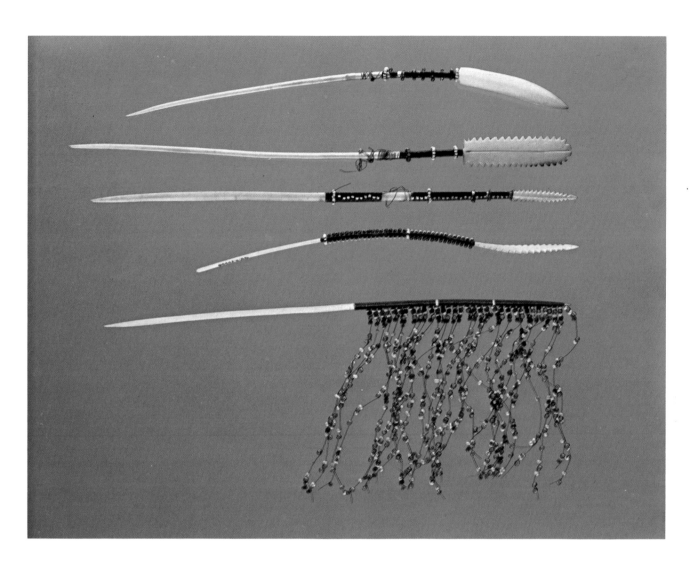

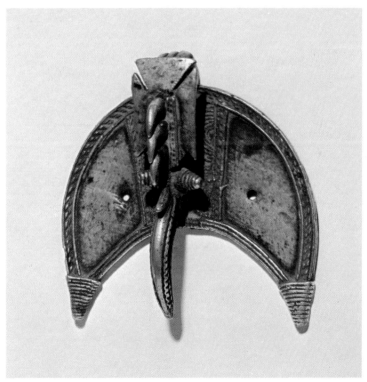

119

left GOLD BEAD. Akan/Baule, Ivory Coast. L. 4 in. Collection Dr. and Mrs. Hilbert H. De-Lawter, Bloomfield Hills, Michigan. Gold was the major prestige metal for groups that were in close contact with the gold fields or lived along the trade routes. Thus, for the Akan peoples, who controlled the gold mines, or for the Sudanic traders, gold was the metal held in highest regard. Elsewhere, even in major kingdoms such as Benin, brass was the metal of royal prerogative.

above HAIR ORNAMENT. Senegal. L. 2¼ in. Collection Dr. and Mrs. Roy Sieber, Blooming-ton, Indiana. A bauble meant to be tied at the forehead where it would peek out from the edge of a head-tie. It is made from base metal, gold-washed.

opposite COMBS. Republic of Zaïre. L. about 7 in. Milwaukee Public Museum. Collected in 1904. Wood and fiber combs, their teeth-splints held parallel to each other by decorative lashings.

JEWELRY is ornament—a valued object worn on the body as adornment or as a badge of distinction. By and large, we in the West consider as ornament that which does not require mutilation of the body in order to support it, although earrings that require the ears to be pierced are an exception. Obviously other societies are not so constrained, and we should consider ear plugs, labrets, nose ornaments, and the like as jewelry. Similarly, when combs and hair- or hatpins are worn as decoration, they should be classified as jewelry—as, perhaps, should whisks and fans.

Early European reports abound in descriptions of necklaces, bracelets, anklets, and rings made of a great variety of materials. Gold was of primary interest, for a major concern of the Europeans on the West Africa coast was the search for this metal, as well as for ivory and spices.[64] Indeed, more jewelry was made of gold, silver, bronze, and copper than in the Congo, east, or south Africa. Casting techniques, especially the lost-wax *(cire-perdue)* process, are known to have been in use in West Africa since the ninth century. On the basis of the sparse evidence we have, casting techniques seem to have come from the north, possibly along the trans-Saharan trade-route system.

Many of the forms of jewelry found in sub-Saharan Africa—particularly where Islam has spread—have parallels in the Mediterranean area and in the Near East. Thus it is possible to draw comparisons between Spanish, Greek, "Arabic," and Ethiopian silver work and the forms and techniques of making silver jewelry in the western Sudan and east Africa.

Early travelers' descriptions would seem to confirm that such influences appeared very early, for cast bracelets and anklets were reported more than 400 years ago. Moreover, the widespread use of stone, bones, tusks, teeth, and shells for beads, and the discovery at Nok of ancient cylindrical double-drilled stone beads,[65] must provoke conjecture of the existence of a premetal jewelry. Further, multistrand necklaces worn by the famous Ife bronze figures of Onis (kings) and the somewhat less well-known Nok terra-cotta figurine of a man (the former 700, the latter 2,000 years old) seem to find a parallel in one worn by the eighteenth-century Gabon king described in Astley: ". . . his Dress [is] different from that of the People; consisting mostly in Beads of Bone and Shells, dyed red, and strung together, like a Chaplet, round his Neck, Arms, and Legs."[66]

Actually we really know very little of the history of jewelry in Africa. It is certain, however, that European glass beads, especially "Venice bugles" (probably millefiori) were in demand as trade items before 1700. On the central Guinea Coast, they were

(continued on page 127)

left COPPER HAIR OR HAT PIN. Republic of Zaïre. L. 19 in. Private collection. Probably from the Kasai region. Pins are most often used by men to anchor small raffia hats to a topknot of hair.

below SILVER HAIRPIN. Bamum, Cameroon. L. 5¼ in. Collection Mrs. Clare K. Gebauer, McMinnville, Oregon. Collected in 1936 in Foumban. The hollow ovate forms at the end of the pin are small lidded containers.

opposite above HAIRPINS. Bihe, Angola. L. 7⅛ in. Royal Ontario Museum, Toronto, Ontario. Would seem to come from the Bihe or related Mbundu (Ovimbundu) peoples of Angola.

opposite below IVORY HAIRPIN. Azande, Republic of Zaïre. L. 11¾ in. Royal Ontario Museum, Toronto, Ontario.

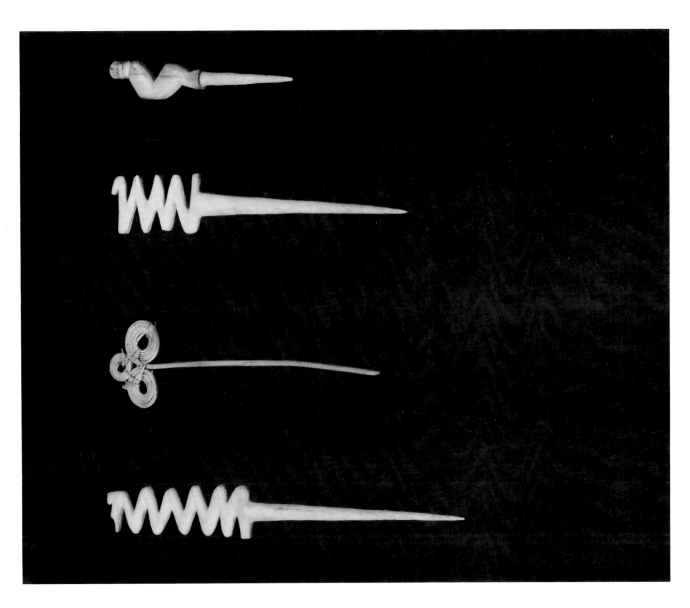

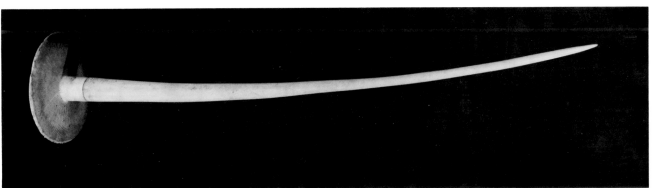

strung with locally produced gold. Barbot, who incorrectly assumed that gold-working techniques had been acquired from earlier Europeans, admired the goldsmiths:

"[They] . . . make of fine gold, breast-plates, helmets, bracelets, idols, hunting-horns, pattins, plates, ornaments for the neck, hatbands, chain and plain rings, buttons, and shell-fish; they also cast very curiously all sorts of wild and tame beasts: the heads and skeletons of lions, tygers, leopards, oxen, deer, monkeys, goats, &c. which serve them by way of idols, either in plain work, or filigrene, all cast in moulds; of which sort I brought over several pieces of figures, but particularly that of a periwinkle, as big as an ordinary goose-egg; which were all much admired at *Rochel* and *Paris,* and even by the best goldsmiths. The thread and contexture of their hatbands and chain-rings is so fine, that I am apt to believe, our ablest *European* artists would find it difficult to imitate them."[67]

Much jewelry is designed to encircle some part of the body: neck, waist, arm, leg, or finger. Illustrated are necklaces (pages 119, 120, 128, 129, 130–141), bangles (pages 143–151), a term taken to include all bracelets and anklets, and rings (pages 137, 152–154).

Only one waist encirclement is illustrated (page 142). In most parts of Africa, waist beads are just that: undifferentiated, undesigned, strings of beads worn about the waist. Perhaps they are best classified as costume rather than jewelry, for they have become a required item of apparel for some groups. They also serve as amulets and are believed to have protective powers. Moreover, they are considered extremely erotic.

above TWO HAIRPINS with beads. Origin unknown. L. 9 in. and 10⅝ in. UCLA Museum of Cultural History, Los Angeles. Gift of George G. Frelinghuysen (above) and the Wellcome trust (below). The hairpin at the top is of bone, its motifs perhaps associated with the Congo River basin or east Africa, and the one below is of iron and is decorated with both seeds and beads.

below RUANDA WOMAN wearing beaded head ornament reserved for Tutsi royalty.

TEXTILES in sub-Saharan Africa are made with few exceptions from vegetable fibers. Wool is rather rare and found mostly in the western Sudan. With the exception of beaten bark cloth, the term "textile" here refers primarily to materials associated with dress, and discussion is limited to cloths woven on looms, omitting netted, knotted, knitted, plaited, and other fabrics.

Textiles of vegetable materials fall into three classes: bark cloth, a nonwoven textile made by beating the inner bark of certain bushes; nonspun fibers, particularly of the raffia palm, which can be woven; and spun fibers, such as cotton. Archaeological evidence indicates that bast (a bundled fiber from bark or stalks) and flat grass fibers were being woven at least as early as a thousand years ago at Igbo-Ukwu in Nigeria. No trace of cotton was found, but the bast yielded a cloth with selvages[68]

(continued on page 155)

NECKLACE. Dogon, Mali. L. 16 in. Collection Dr. and Mrs. Marshall W. Mount, New York. Barbot (1732, p. 62) described necklaces of protective *grigris* (leather amulets) enclosing verses copied from the Koran. The amulets in this necklace are combined with yellow amber (which Barbot listed as a major item of currency imported by European traders), European silver coins, and red glass beads that resemble coral, another highly prized import.

128

above BRASS PENDANT. Bobo, Upper Volta. L.
4½ in. Collection Jay T. Last, Los Angeles. The
form is that of a male leopard with prey.

below BRASS PENDANT. Origin unknown. L.

5 in. Collection Mr. and Mrs. Irwin Hersey,
New York. The shape seems to represent a
hornbill, a bird of great ritual significance
among several groups in the Ivory Coast and
Upper Volta.

above BRASS AND BEAD NECKLACE. Kru, Liberia, or Ngere, Ivory Coast. D. 16 in. Private collection. Cast-brass imitations of leopard's teeth intermixed with brass beads and bells and blue-glass beads. A similar necklace, but with real teeth, is described by Barbot (1732, p. 125); it was worn by a youth at his emergence as an adult from the initiation school.

opposite GOLD brought out of Africa by Europeans was in three forms: dust, nuggets, and "fetish gold." Early travelers' reports used the latter term to describe the ornaments worked into hair and beards and the gold necklaces and bangles worn by African princes.

above COPPER PENDANT. Akan/Baule, Ivory Coast. H. 3¼ in. Collection Mr. and Mrs. Ernst Anspach, New York. A pendant in the form of a human face.

below GOLD PENDANT. Akan/Baule or Ebrie, Ivory Coast. D. 1¾ in. The Museum of Primitive Art, New York. Gift of René d'Harnoncourt. A pendant in the form of a snake.

above GOLD PENDANT DISK. Akan/Baule, Ivory Coast. D. 2⅜ in. Collection Mrs. Harry A. Franklin, Beverly Hills, California.

below GOLD PENDANT. Akan/Baule, Ivory Coast. L. 3 in. Collection Katherine White Reswick, Los Angeles. A pendant in the form of a crocodile.

131

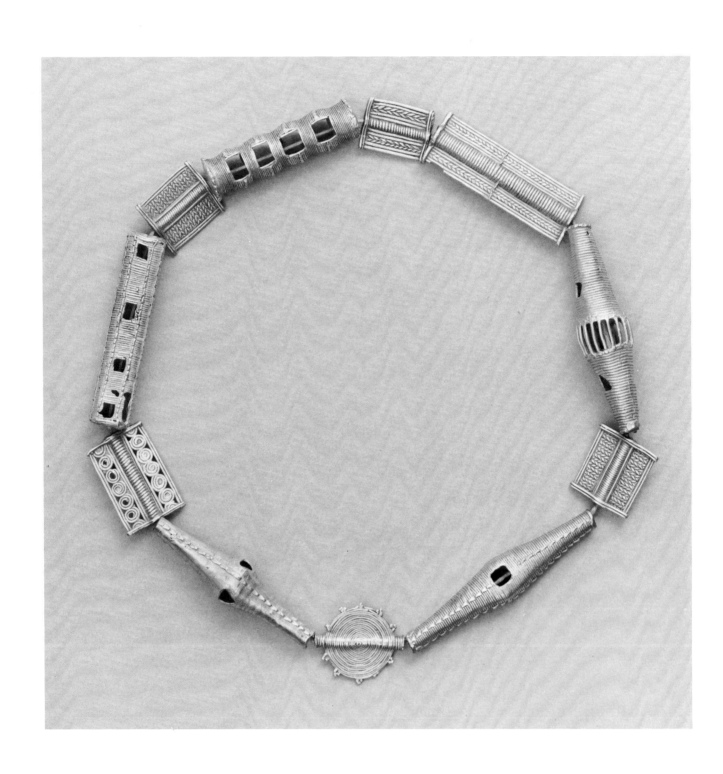

GOLD NECKLACE. Akan/Ashanti, Ghana. L. 15¼ in. The Museum of Primitive Art, New York. Barbot (1732, p. 238) in his description of the apparel of women stated: "...about their necks they wear gold chains...besides ten or twelve other strings of gold, or coral, which adorn their arms, waist and legs, so thick, especially about their waist, that had they no other clothes or girdles about it, they would suffice to cover what modesty ought to conceal."

BRASS NECK RING. Bamum, Cameroon. D. 11 in.
Private collection. A prestige ornament consisting of a brass circlet with thirty bushcow
heads formed through the lost-wax process.

left above WOODEN NECK RING. Cameroon. D. 9¾ in. University Museum, Philadelphia.

left center BRASS NECK RING. Fang, Gabon. D. 8 in. The Cleveland Museum of Art, Rockefeller Grant. Metal neck rings from the equatorial forests of the southern Cameroons, Gabon, and the northwest Congo River basin were usually associated with marriage and were worn permanently.

left below COPPER PENDANT. Republic of Zaïre. W. 8¼ in. University Museum, Philadelphia. Collected by Leo Frobenius in 1906.

opposite COPPER NECK RING. Bwaka, Republic of Zaïre. D. 8½ in. The Peabody Museum, Harvard University, Cambridge, Massachusetts. Collected about 1890.

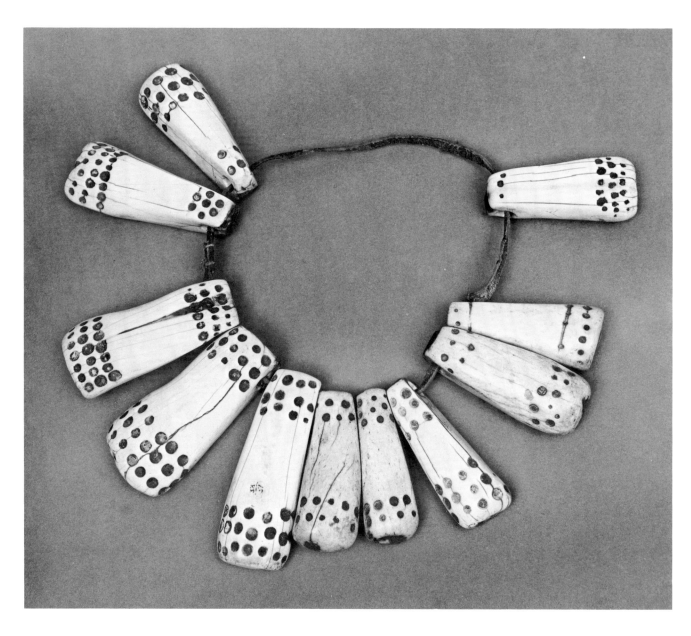

above IVORY NECKLACE. Republic of Zaïre (?). L. each bead 5 in. UCLA Museum of Cultural History, Los Angeles. Gift of the Wellcome trust.

right above GOLD RING. Akan/Ashanti, Ghana. H. 1¾ in. The Cleveland Museum of Art. Purchase from the J. H. Wade Fund. A type of ring associated with royal regalia among the Akan. The snake probably refers to a proverb pertaining to leadership.

right below GLASS RING. Nupe, Bida, Nigeria. D. 1½ in. Private collection. Nupe glass rings are far rarer than bracelets or beads. Originally the glass was produced at Bida; now imported glass bottles are used.

far right above GOLD PENDANT. Akan/Baule, Ivory Coast. H. 3½ in. The Museum of Primitive Art, New York. A pendant in the form of a human face.

far right below GOLD SOUL DISK. Akan/Ashanti, Ghana. D. 3¹³⁄₁₆ in. The Cleveland Museum of Art, Dudley P. Allen Fund. From the treasury of King Prempeh. The badge of a priest who was responsible for the purity of the Asantehene's soul. The state of well-being of the kingdom was believed to be directly related to the condition of the soul of the king.

NECKPIECE. Tutsi, Rwanda. D. 8 in. UCLA Museum of Cultural History, Los Angeles. Made of goatskin covered with black and white beads and fringed with the white hair of a Colobus monkey.

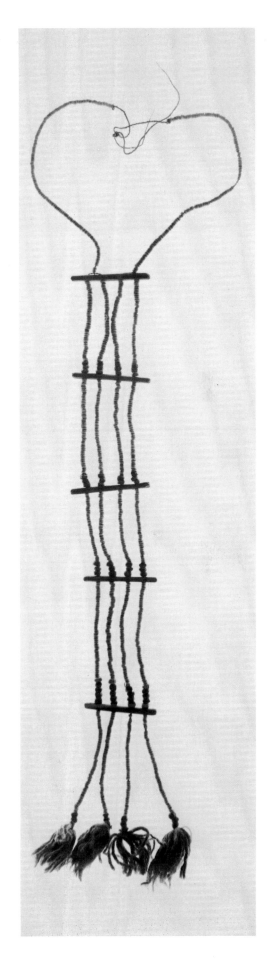

above NECKLACE. Ikoma, Tanzania. D. 9 in. Milwaukee Public Museum. Collected in 1929. Made of beetle-wing covers.

right NECKLACE. Ambo, Southwest Africa. L. 19 in. R. H. Lowie Museum of Anthropology, Berkeley, California. Collected in 1947/48. Made of shells, beads, tassels, and wood, and reported to have come from the Kuanyama, a subgroup of the Ambo or Ovambo, who live in a territory covering part of both Angola and Southwest Africa.

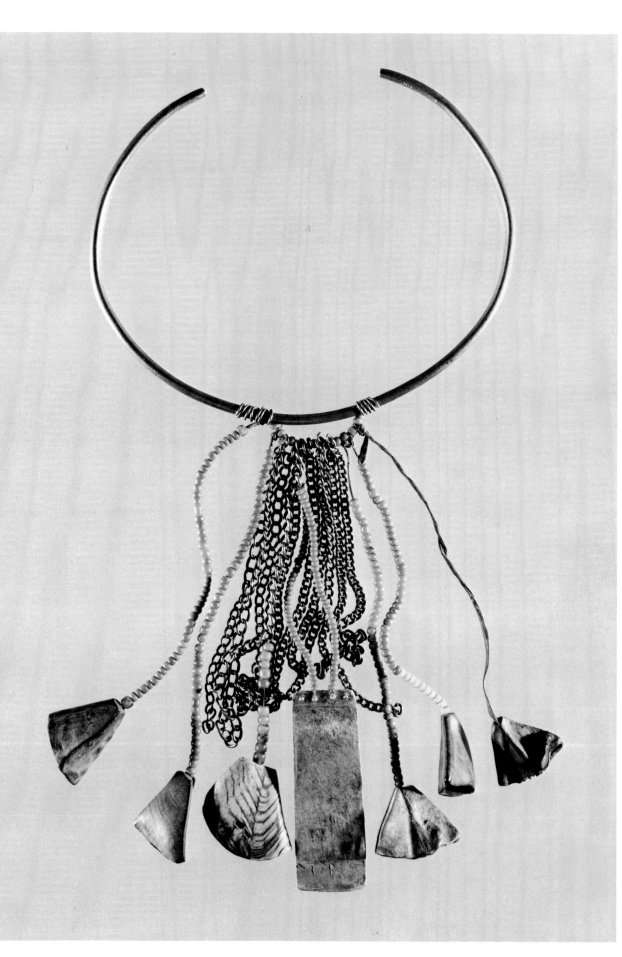

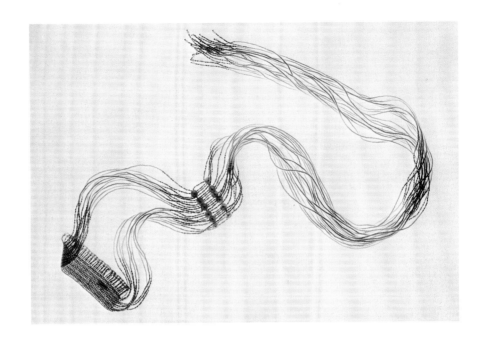

opposite NECKLACE. Pokot, Kenya. D. 6 in. The American Museum of Natural History, New York. Collected in 1963. An open wire circlet, worn by women and young girls, decorated with a chain and bead fringe and the claws of an anteater.

above BEAD NECKLACE. Nguni, South Africa. L. 50 in. R. H. Lowie Museum of Anthropology, Berkeley, California. Collected in 1968. Worn by young men.

below BEAD NECKLACE. Origin unknown. L. of unit 4½ in. The Peabody Museum of Salem, Massachusetts.

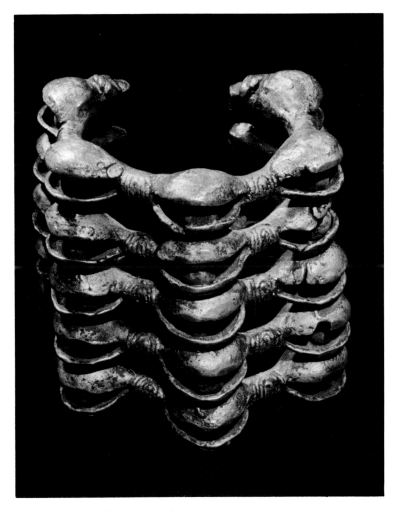

opposite WAIST ORNAMENT. Vai, Liberia. D. 12½ in. The Peabody Museum, Harvard University, Cambridge, Massachusetts. Collected by George Schwab in 1927. This body circlet of glass and brass beads and a brass frontpiece was worn by a woman under her clothing. It is a form of private ornament, never to be displayed in public.

above BRASS BRACELET. Upper Volta. D. 4¼ in. Private collection. A lost-wax casting that seems to derive from forged examples in which the bar of metal is twisted or knotted. At times such bangles are associated with healing rituals.

below BRASS ANKLET. Gio, Liberia. D. 5 in. Collection Mr. and Mrs. William M. Taylor, Washington, D.C. Cast as a single unit, this anklet simulates an accumulation of five bangles, each with five bells.

above GOLD OBJECT. Akan/Ashanti, Ghana. W.
1⅞ in. UCLA Museum of Cultural History, Los
Angeles. Gift of the Wellcome trust. Collected
in 1874. Perhaps a bracelet, but more likely
used to decorate some piece of apparel. It is
probably the best example of Ashanti floral
motifs in gold repoussé on this continent.

below BRASS ANKLET. Kru, Ivory Coast (?). W.
9¼ in. Collection Katherine White Reswick,
Los Angeles. An exceptionally large anklet
weighing fourteen pounds.

opposite BRASS BRACELET. Nigeria. D. 4 in. Collection Mr. and Mrs. J. Newton Hill, New York.
A cast-brass bangle; may be ascribed to the
Lower Niger Bronze Industry, a cumbersome
designation for a group of bronze or brass objects of uncertain date in several styles that are
clearly distinct from those of ancient Ife or
Benin and the modern Yoruba. The detail of
this piece relates it to works widely found in
southwestern Nigeria.

GLASS ARMLET. Nupe, Bida, Nigeria. D. 6 in. Collection Dr. and Mrs. Roy Sieber, Bloomington, Indiana. Bracelet from the Nupe, one of two African groups that traditionally manufactured and worked glass (the other is the Fanti of Ghana). This may be a copy of a type of stone bracelet that originated in northern Ghana and traveled the pre-European kola-nut trade route to northern Nigeria.

COPPER ANKLET. Fulani (?), Nigeria. D. 5½ in. Collection Dr. and Mrs. Roy Sieber, Bloomington, Indiana. A twisted and forged copper bar ornamented with punchwork. Its form and decoration are based on Islamic prototypes.

BRASS ANKLET. Kapsiki, Cameroon. D. 5½ in. Collection Dr. and Mrs. Marshall W. Mount, New York. Collected in 1969 in Rumsiki town. The numerous small groups of hill peoples of the northern Cameroon, including the Kapsiki, continue to be called Kirdi, although nearly 150 years ago Denham (1826, p. 111) corrected this error. "Kirdi" is a pejorative term applied by the Islamic slave traders to unbelievers.

IRON ANKLET. Basa, Cameroon. D. 5 in. The Peabody Museum, Harvard University, Cambridge, Massachusetts. Collected by George W. Schwab in 1922. A leg ornament in the form of a rattle; from the forest area of southern Cameroon.

COPPER ANKLETS. Republic of Zaïre. D. 4½ in. University Museum, Philadelphia. Reported to have come from the Stanley Falls region of the Congo River. It is often impossible to judge from museum or field descriptions whether particular types of objects are worn by men or women or both. In this instance, an old photograph shows anklets of this sort worn by women, although the particular ethnic group is not identified. (In *Le Miroir du Congo Belge,* 1929, vol. 1, p. 111).

COPPER ANKLET. Republic of Zaïre. H. 6½ in. Buffalo Museum of Science. Collected before 1900. Said to have come from the Tshauppa River region of north-central Zaïre. Puddle-cast in an open mold, the anklet was shaped by pounding.

IVORY BANGLE. Origin unknown. L. 7 in. Milwaukee Public Museum. Ivory is used throughout sub-Saharan Africa for bracelets and anklets in a variety of forms and styles.

BRACELET, wood with copper inlay. Rwanda. D. 8½ in. Collection Dr. Daniel P. Biebuyck, Newark, Delaware. A wrist protector used by archers and invariably shown worn on the left wrist in photographs of Tutsi chiefs.

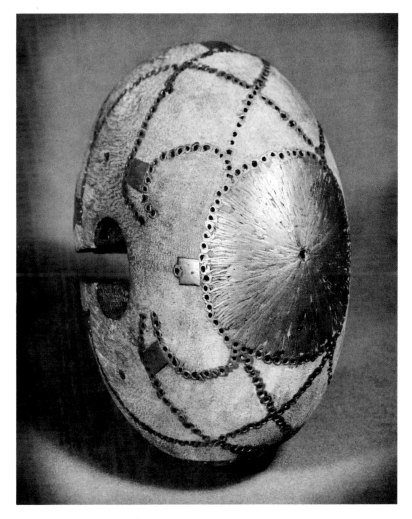

opposite COILED-WIRE BANGLE. Masai, Kenya or Tanzania. H. 8 in. R. H. Lowie Museum of Anthropology, Berkeley, California. Collected in 1947/48. Worn by women on wrists and ankles.

above WOOD ARMLET. Masai, Kenya or Tanzania. W. 6½ in. The Museum of Primitive Art, New York. Worn by men on the upper arm above the biceps with points upward.

below BRASS RING. Bobo, Upper Volta. H. 2¼ in. Collection Jay T. Last, Los Angeles. Collected in Touziana village. Lost-wax casting in the form of an equestrian figure, unusually sculptural in concept.

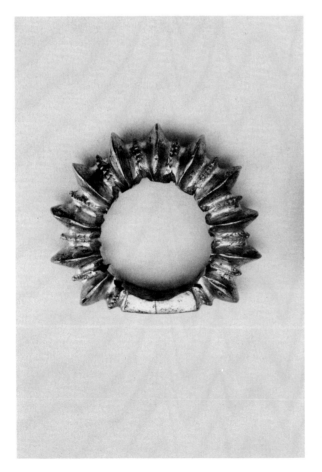

left above BRASS DOUBLE RING. Bobo, Upper Volta. W. 4¼ in. Collection Jay T. Last, Los Angeles.

left below SILVER RING. Upper Volta. D. 1½ in. Private collection. Silver ring in style found from Senegal to Ethiopia. Some rings of this type are meant to be worn on the left thumb to ward off disease.

right above BRASS RING. Ghana or Upper Volta. D. 1⅛ in. Collection Dr. and Mrs. Franklin Williams, New York. A copy of a coin ring.

far right above BRASS RING. Ghana or Upper Volta. L. 1⅝ in. Collection Mrs. Genevieve McMillan, Cambridge, Massachusetts. Cast by the lost-wax technique. A real peanut attached to a wax ring was encased in clay and heated to melt the wax and burn off the peanut. The resulting cavity was filled with molten brass.

right below BRASS RING. Ghana (?). D. 1¾ in. Mrs. Genevieve McMillan, Cambridge, Massachusetts. The sandals depicted on this ring resemble some Ashanti gold weights; however, the type of sandals and the character of the casting are too general to assign the ring with certainty to Ghana.

far right below BRASS RING. Senufo, Ivory Coast. H. 1⅞ in. Collection Jay T. Last, Los Angeles. The form is that of a chameleon, an animal important in the creation myth of the Senufo. From the Nafana area.

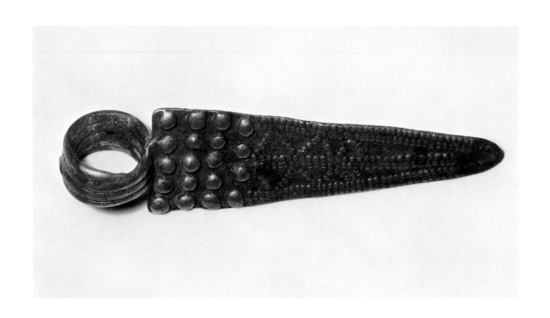

that may have been woven on a loom. Evidence exists that cotton was in use at Benin in Nigeria by the thirteenth century.[69] Textiles were very likely produced on the loom even earlier than either of these dates. At the same time the dates do establish that textiles were produced well before European contacts.

Beaten bark cloth was at one time in use over much of the subcontinent. It was reported in Liberia as early as the middle of the sixteenth century,[70] and in the more recent past in Uganda (page 157, top) and the central Congo, or Zaïre (pages 157, bottom; 159). It is known today in Ghana and Nigeria.[71] It may be cut and sewn as patchwork, embroidered, and painted (pages 156, 158, 159). It is, however, quite fragile, particularly if wet, and when stronger fabrics become available, they tend to replace it.

To understand the nature, character, and aesthetic of African loomed textiles, it is necessary to realize that several types of looms exist, each producing a characteristic cloth. In West Africa, two are clearly distinguishable: a fixed-frame, treadleless, heddle-stick (sword), comparatively wide vertical loom, used by women, and a double-heddle, narrow-band, horizontal treadle loom, used by men (pages 160, 161, top).

The piece of cloth produced on the woman's vertical loom is approximately twice the size of its work area, for the warp threads go over the top and bottom supports in a continuous spiral. Women are weavers by avocation; in many areas, nearly every woman weaves for her own and her family's use, and only excess cloths are sold or bartered. The woven pieces are either used just as they come from the loom or two or three may be edge-sewn to produce a single large cloth. Traditionally, the "women's weaves" are never cut or tailored; the cloths are used for the mantle and wraparound costume described earlier.

In contrast, the man's horizontal loom produces an extremely long, narrow strip of cloth. It is, indeed, theoretically endless. The men weavers are specialists who have undergone an apprenticeship, making cloth exclusively for sale. The narrow strips are edge-sewn to produce larger cloths that may be used as mantles, wraparounds, and blankets, but more usually are tailored.

Where the narrow strip loom is found, it is always used by men. In West Africa, the vertical loom is used solely by women. However, in other parts of Africa—particularly in the Congo River basin—where the strip loom is not found, the men use the vertical loom to produce raffia cloth (page 161, bottom). This suggests that in earlier times the vertical loom was used by men, primarily for weaving raffia, but that later, when the strip loom

(continued on page 159)

left BEATEN BARK CLOTH. Kuba, Republic of Zaïre. 58½ x 27½ in. Indiana University Art Museum, Bloomington. Patchwork skirt of bark cloth and European cloth with a raffia border in overstitched embroidery. This garment joins several materials and techniques in a prestige dress.

opposite above BEATEN BARK CLOTH. Uganda. 83½ x 69¼ in. Department of Art, Fisk University, Nashville, Tennessee. Collected in 1931. The inner bark of certain trees, when beaten, produces a fine, soft material, once widely used in nearly all of sub-Saharan Africa. Because it is not woven, designs must be painted or stamped on.

opposite below BEATEN BARK CLOTH. Kuba, Republic of Zaïre. 24 x 11 in. Minnesota Museum of Art, St. Paul. A skirt of patchwork bark cloth.

left BEATEN BARK CLOTH with raffia embroidery. Tanzania. 54 x 32 in. Field Museum of Natural History, Chicago. Gift of Mrs. A. W. Fuller.

opposite BEATEN BARK CLOTH. Pygmy, Ituri Forest, Republic of Zaïre. 18 x 23 in. Field Museum of Natural History, Chicago. Collected in 1959. A bark-cloth skirt with painted designs.

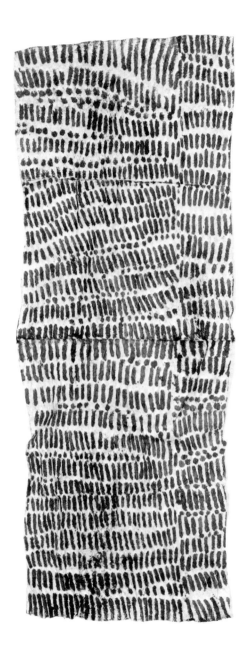

was introduced from the north,[72] the vertical loom became the women's tool. Other than in the doubling, which nonspun raffia fibers are too short to allow, the raffia loom of the Gabon and the Congo closely resembles the vertical loom of West Africa.

The raffia loom permits the manufacture of small pieces of cloth, or mats, usually without a selvage. Most raffia cloths are therefore overlapped and sewn to make larger pieces, and the edges hemmed. Raffia cloth was reported from most of the West Coast quite early. Barbot recorded it on the Ivory Coast,[73] others on the Congo coast.[74]

Barbot described four types of raffia cloth from the Kingdom of the Kongo in the eighteenth century. The finest, never sold, was made solely for the king. Two other types were for sale; one of the two, "for the greatest noblemen, [was] made very fine, and with curious workmanship, flower'd, and beautify'd with exquisite imagery, each cloth holding about two spans and a half [about ten inches] square, which a weaver with his greatest diligence may well spend fifteen or sixteen days in working to finish it."[75] Finally, plain-woven cloths in contrast to the "high and cut work" of the finer sorts were used for trade and worn by commoners and slaves. The fine cloths have been preserved in a very few examples, including two, recently identified, in the British Museum, London. They were part of the original Sir Hans Sloane collection and therefore were brought to Europe before 1750.[76]

Cloths of fine raffia and of raffia and cotton are woven today in Dahomey (pages 162, 164), Nigeria, and the Republic of Zaïre (page 165). Subtle patterns may be introduced in the weaving or additive techniques such as embroidery and appliqué may be used to enhance the basic ground.

In the Kasai area of the Republic of Zaïre and particularly among the Kuba, impressive raffia cloths are produced jointly by men and women, with the men making the basic mats and the women sewing and embroidering the designs. Palm-leaf fibers, stripped, rubbed, and scraped, are woven into mats by men working on vertical looms. The finished mat may be placed in a mortar with cold water and beaten with a smooth ivory pestle to soften it.[77] The mats, hemmed and stitched together, serve at times as a base for appliqué (page 166). A description dating from early in the century suggests that "holes and worn places . . . were skillfully covered by pieces appliquéd on in different designs with palm fiber dyed black."[78]

Alternatively, the cloth may be embroidered: openwork (page 167), oversewing (page 168, bottom), and cut-pile (page 169) techniques are used. Cut-pile cloths, the so-called Kasai velvets,

(continued on page 163)

left WOMAN'S LOOM, Okene, Nigeria. The vertical loom for weaving cotton or, more rarely, raffia is the sort used by women in West Africa. The warp threads are wrapped over the upper and lower support bars; thus the finished cloth is twice the size of the working face.

opposite above MEN'S LOOMS, Katiorokpo village, Senufo, Ivory Coast. The horizontal strip loom with a single pair of heddles is invariably used by men in West Africa. Senufo weavers are a special caste whose wives are potters.

opposite below MAN'S VERTICAL RAFFIA LOOM, Kuba, Republic of Zaïre. Unlike the women's vertical loom farther west, this raffia loom produces a single mat, usually without selvages.

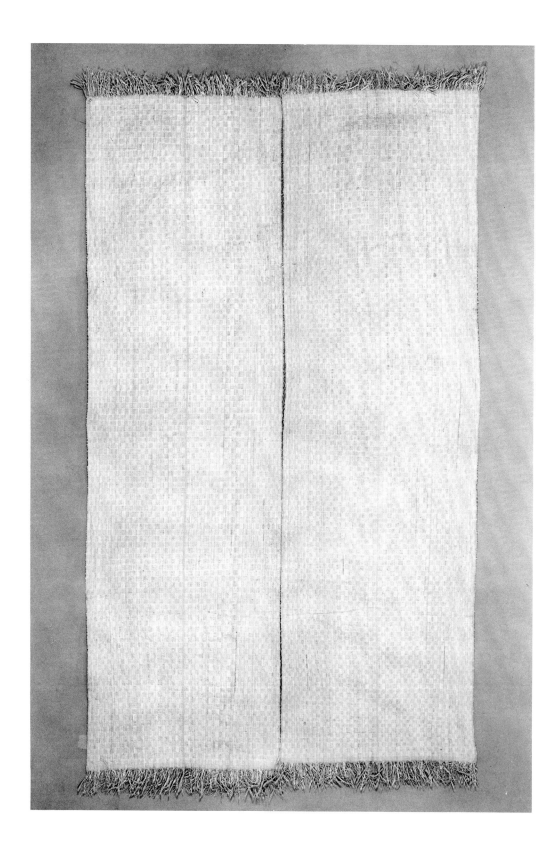

are among the best known African prestige cloths.[79] The designs are relatively varied and fairly complex; each pattern has a name and a symbolic meaning. These velvets are worn as high-prestige costume, and their richness and variety are a clear indication of the great value traditionally placed on them.

William H. Sheppard described the technique for cut pile. The mat serves as a foundation that "is then worked in designs with a needle and palm thread, a small sharp knife being used to clip off the tufts. They do not mark the design but keep the pattern in their heads."[80]

The oral history of this form of cloth-making was recorded by Emil Torday,[81] who reported that the Mbala subgroup traces the origins of the technique to a culture hero, possibly of the seventeenth century. This king, Shamba Bulongongo (more recently spelled Shyaam aMbul aNgoong),[82] is said to have traveled westward and returned with the craft. Torday thought he had gone to the Pende, but possibly he traveled as far as the Kingdom of Kongo. The basic cut-pile technique used today among the Kuba resembles that of eighteenth-century examples.

In West Africa the women, working on a vertical loom, weave predominantly with cotton, although raffia in conjunction with cotton does appear. The width of the cloths ranges from sixteen to twenty inches, and the length from forty-eight to seventy-two inches. Because the threads are doubled over the top and bottom warp beams, the working face or area of the warp is about sixteen by twenty-four to thirty-six inches. As the work progresses, the finished cloth is slipped down over the lower warp beam and up the back, thus keeping the shed and shuttle at approximately chest level (page 160).

A string-loop heddle bar and a shed stick permit only a rather laborious tenting of the warp fibers. Nevertheless, this comparatively slow weaving process results in amazingly handsome cloths. A simple warp stripe, often of indigo and white homespun, depends on a monochrome weft (page 168, top); if the warp and weft are striped, a plaid results (page 171, bottom). Solid-color baby cloths, used to anchor a baby on its mother's back, may have a looped weft (page 171, top). Whatever the pattern or weave, baby cloths are worn with the tufted or looped side out, and not, as one might expect, against the baby. When the weave is compacted so that the weft stripes are hidden, subtle variations in the warp striping may result (page 172).

Extra heddle bars may be added to allow for the development of brocade patterns. These patterns, usually in contrasting colors and often of different fibers, are the result, almost invariably, of added wefts; that is, they are not a part of the basic warp and

RITUAL MARRIAGE CLOTH, raffia and cotton. Fon, Dahomey. 63 x 37 in. The Herskovits Collection, Evanston, Illinois.

(continued on page 170)

163

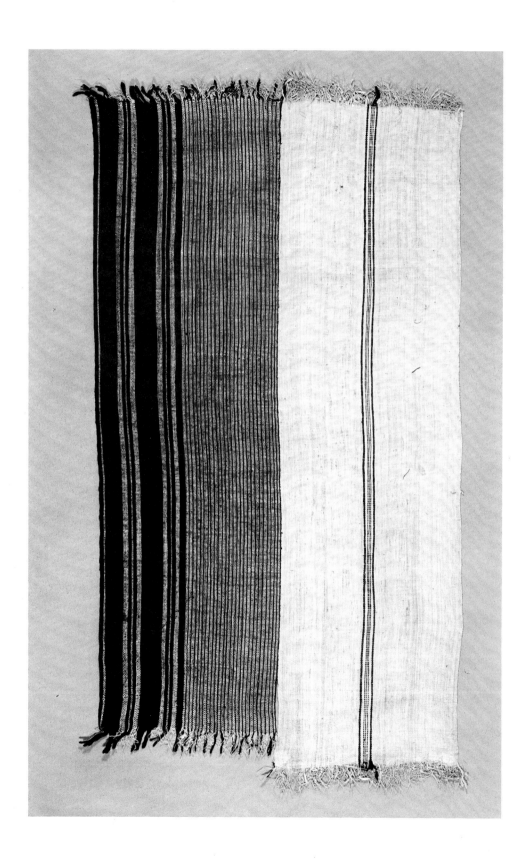

opposite FUNERAL CLOTH, raffia and cotton. Fon, Dahomey. 63 x 37 in. The Herskovits Collection, Evanston, Illinois. Dahomey has been well-known for fine cotton and raffia cloths since the early eighteenth century.

right RAFFIA CLOTH. Teke, Republic of Zaïre. 86 x 38 in. Field Museum of Natural History, Chicago. Collected in 1903. Small pieces are sewed together to form this mantle for a chief.

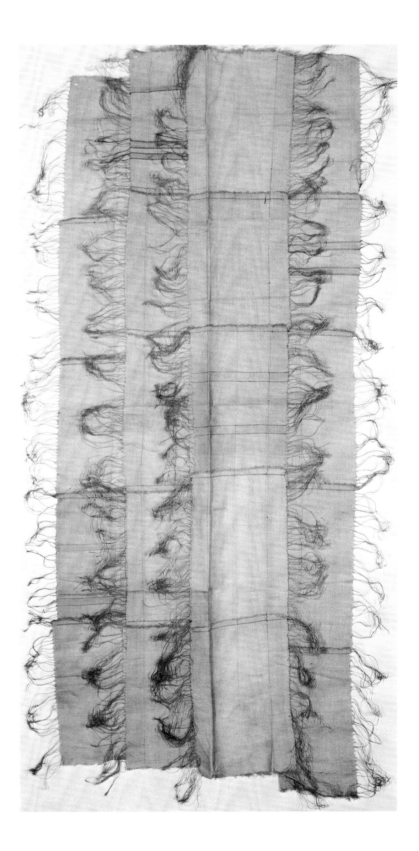

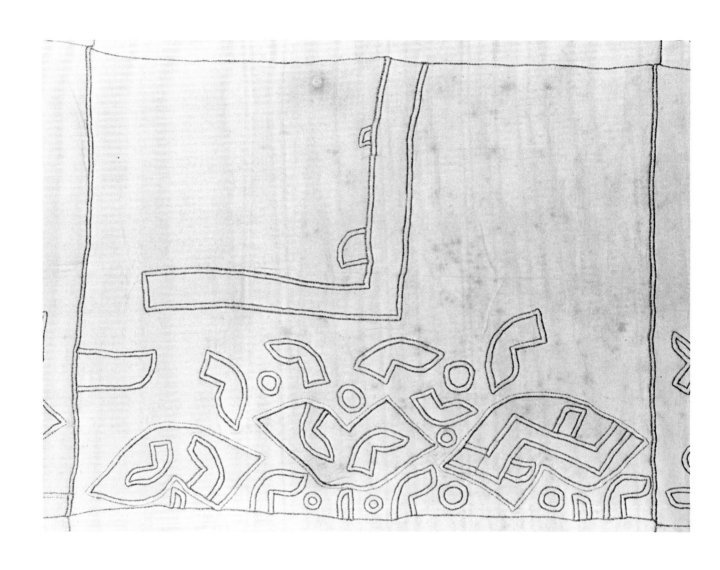

above WOMAN'S RAFFIA WRAPAROUND. Kuba, Republic of Zaïre. 17 ft., 3 in. x 24 in. The College Museum, Hampton Institute, Hampton, Virginia. Collected by William H. Sheppard about 1900. Extremely soft raffia matting with an appliqué of the same material to hide holes produced by pounding the mats to soften them.

opposite MAN'S RAFFIA WRAPAROUND (fragment). Kuba, Republic of Zaïre. Original garment was 30 ft. x 29 in. Minnesota Museum of Art, St. Paul. Collected early in this century, this exceptional piece is reputed to have then been more than a hundred years old. The openwork embroidery is contained within a border of overstitching and a fringe of raffia balls. Probably from the Mbala subtribe of the Kuba.

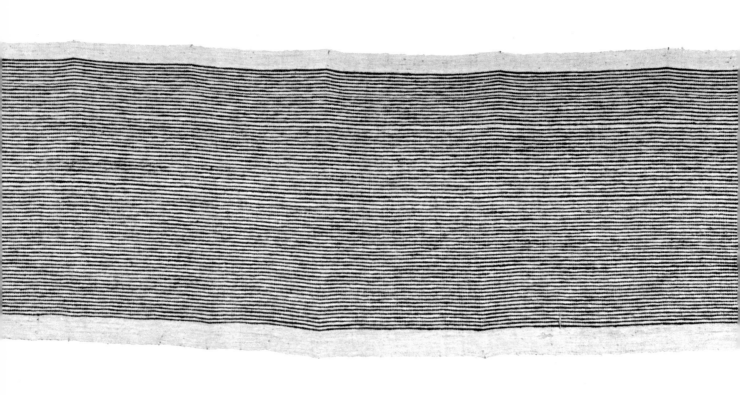

opposite above WOMEN'S WEAVE. Yoruba, Nigeria. 54 x 16 in. Collection Dr. and Mrs. Roy Sieber, Bloomington, Indiana. White and indigo cloth of locally grown and spun cotton woven on a woman's vertical loom. Probably from the northern Yoruba.

opposite below EMBROIDERED RAFFIA MAT. Kuba (?), Republic of Zaïre. 23 x 11 in. Collection Jack Lenor Larsen, New York. Embroidered by women using iron needles. A variety of techniques are used, including oversewing, as here, openwork, eyelet or buttonhole stitching, and most spectacularly, a form of cut-pile work.

right CUT-PILE-EMBROIDERED RAFFIA CLOTH. Kuba, Republic of Zaïre. 27 x 13¾ in. Collection Mr. and Mrs. William Bascom, Berkeley, California. Collected in 1943.

weft structure of the cloth, but ride on one surface, locked in place by some warp threads. Spectacular and at times gaudy brocaded women's weaves have been developed in two towns in Nigeria: Okene, north of Benin, and Akwete in Iboland; both are quite famous for high fashion cloths that have become popular, expensive prestige costume (pages 173, bottom; 174–177). Similar cloths with brocaded patterns are woven by Nupe women (page 178).

More mundane, but not necessarily pedestrian, blankets or wrappers are produced at Kano and elsewhere in northern Nigeria (pages 179, 180, 182).

One may infer from the report of Cado Mosto that the men's horizontal strip loom was in use as early as 1455 on the Senegal coast: "They weave pieces of cotton a span wide, but never any wider, not having the art of making larger looms; so that they are obliged to sew five or six of these pieces together, when they make any large work."[83]

Barbot probably derived the following description of weaving from an earlier seventeenth-century source. "The Weavers are the most numerous among the mechanicks, and would make very good cloth had they large looms; but they wholly apply themselves to weaving of a narrow, thick, striped cotton-cloth, seven or eight fingers broad, and about two ells and a half long, in small portable looms, made for that purpose. They afterwards stitch together six, seven, or eight of those narrow slips to make a cloth or *Panho*, as they have learned to call it from the *Portuguese*."[84] The cloth he described was approximately nine by three feet, a not unusual size today. A later report (1738) noted that the strips "are generally twenty seven Yards long and never above 9 inches wide. . . ."[85] From this, two cloths could be made: one, nine by four-and-a-half feet, for use as a mantle, and the other, six by four-and-a-half feet, as a waistcloth. This was the basic costume—as noted—for men and women, not only in the region of the Gambia River,[86] but for most of the West African coast.

The early traveler Paul Erdman Isert explicitly describes narrow-band weaving on a horizontal loom by the Akreen on the Gold Coast in the late eighteenth century.[87]

The wide distribution of striped cloths made on the horizontal strip loom reflects their popularity. It is clear from early reports that the Portuguese and later merchants used them as trade items up and down the coast. *Panhos* are mentioned in many descriptions, and it is certain that in the Cape Verde Islands and on the mainland of the Senegal coast, cloths were produced in great quantity to be used as currency.[88] Also, by the early eigh-

(continued on page 181)

above WOMEN'S WEAVE. Yoruba, Nigeria. 70 x 15 in. Collection Carl and Joanne Eicher, East Lansing, Michigan. Collected in Abeokuta. Baby tie worn by the mother over other clothing to support a baby on her back. The looped weft is worn outside, not against the child, and is decorative rather than functional.

below WOMEN'S WEAVE. Yoruba, Nigeria. 92 x 40 in. Collection Mrs. Mary S. Thieme, Nashville, Tennessee. Collected in Ado Ekiti in 1965. A simple plaid of homespun indigo and white cotton.

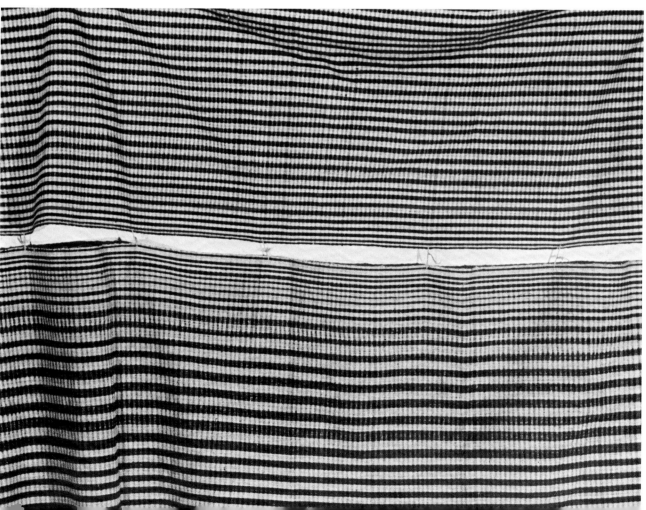

above WOMEN'S WEAVE. Ibo, Nigeria. 48 x 15 in. Collection Mr. and Mrs. Simon Ottenberg, Seattle. The arrangement of red and white warp threads allows this apparently complicated weave to emerge quite simply with a red weft (warp face warp stripe).

opposite above WOMEN'S WEAVE. Yoruba, Nigeria. 80 x 58 in. Collection Katherine White Reswick, Los Angeles. Collected in Owo. Produced on a wide loom, it nevertheless resembles the designs of men's weaving. The tie dyeing of

some of the warp threads—a warp *ikat*—creates a blue-white alternation that modifies the intensity of the warp stripes.

opposite below WOMEN'S WEAVE. Okene, Nigeria. 71 x 50 in. Collection Kay L. McGlachlin, Los Angeles. The basic women's weave may be enhanced with a brocade of supplementary wefts in a contrasting thread. At Okene, north of Benin, the Edo women have produced a characteristic style of cloth that has become a major prestige textile throughout much of Nigeria.

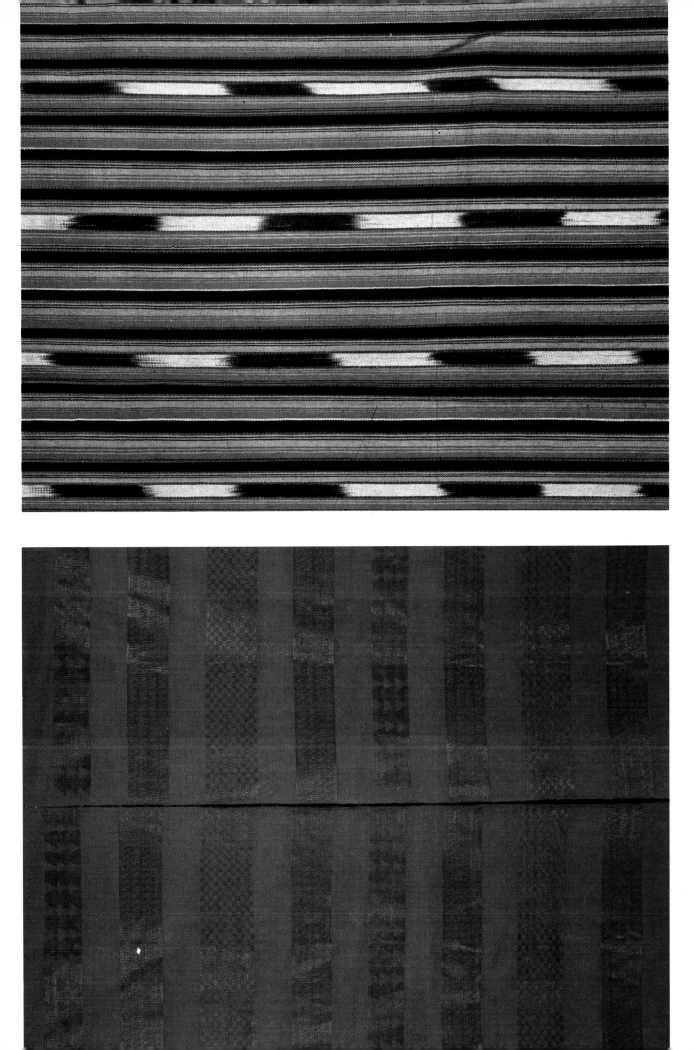

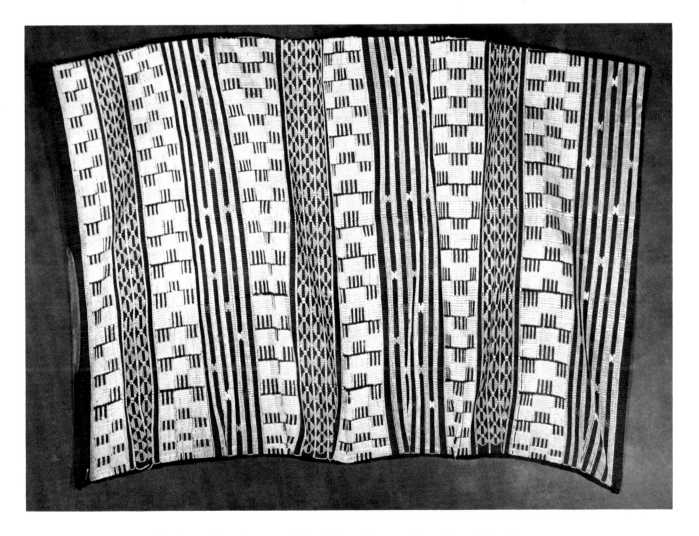

above WOMEN'S WEAVE *(detail opposite)*. Ibo, Akwete, Nigeria. 72 x 60 in. Collection Mr. and Mrs. Herbert M. Cole, Santa Barbara, Calif. Akwete, in southeastern Nigeria, is another center for highly developed brocade and prestige cloths woven by women.

below WOMEN'S WEAVE. Ibo, Akwete, Nigeria. 64 x 41 in. Collection Bill and Alfredine Brown, Hillcrest Heights, Maryland. A cloth in black, yellow, and red on a white base.

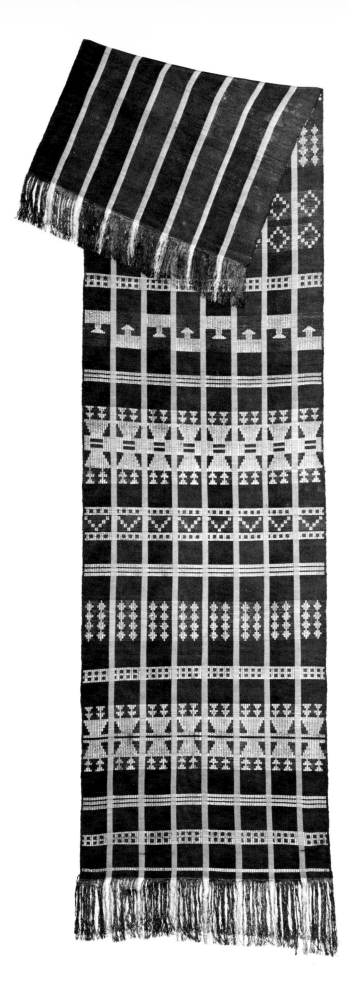

opposite WOMEN'S WEAVE. Ibo, Akwete, Nigeria. 67 x 47 in. Collection Dr. Janet A. Hartle, Washington, D.C.

right WOMEN'S WEAVE. Okene, Nigeria. 105 x 18 in. Department of Anthropology, University of Denver. Collected by Kate P. Kent. A brocade of gold silk supplementary weft threads over green, yellow, and blue stripes.

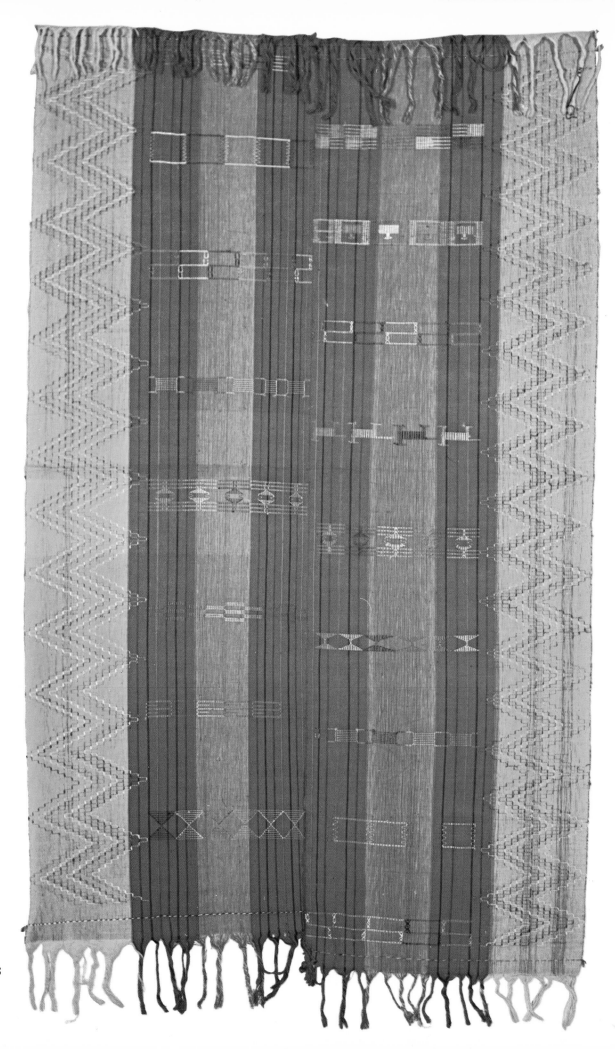

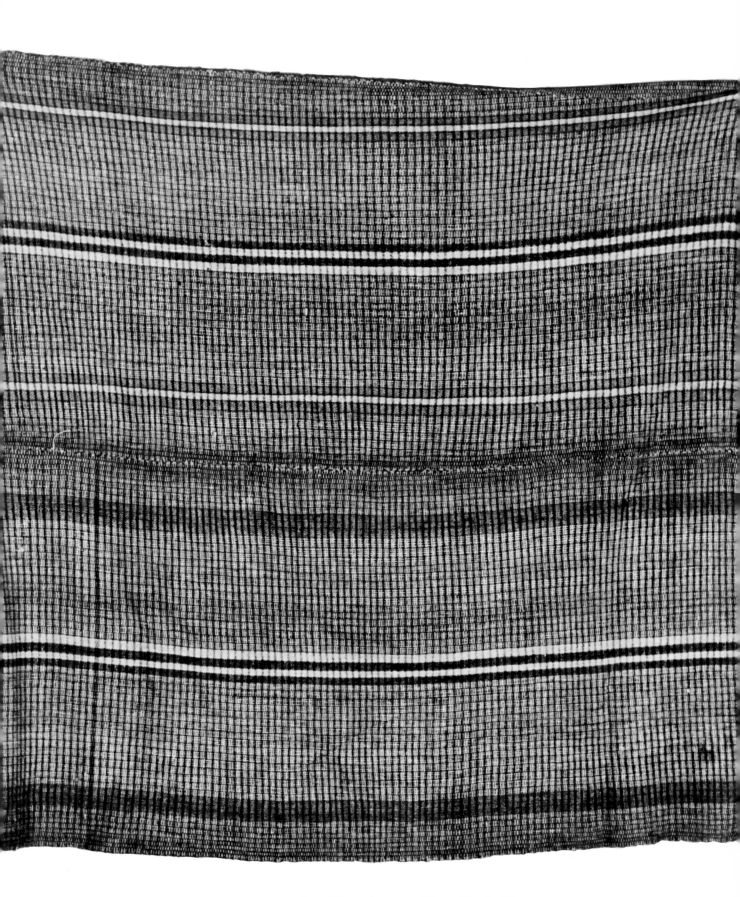

opposite WOMEN'S WEAVE. Nupe, Bida, Nigeria. 74 x 49 in. Collection Professor and Mrs. Robert Farris Thompson, Hamden, Connecticut.

above WOMEN'S WEAVE. Hausa, Nigeria. 72 x 42 in. Collection Mrs. Mary S. Thieme, Nashville, Tennessee. Collected in 1965. This cloth and the three that follow are primarily of indigo and white with added color touches.

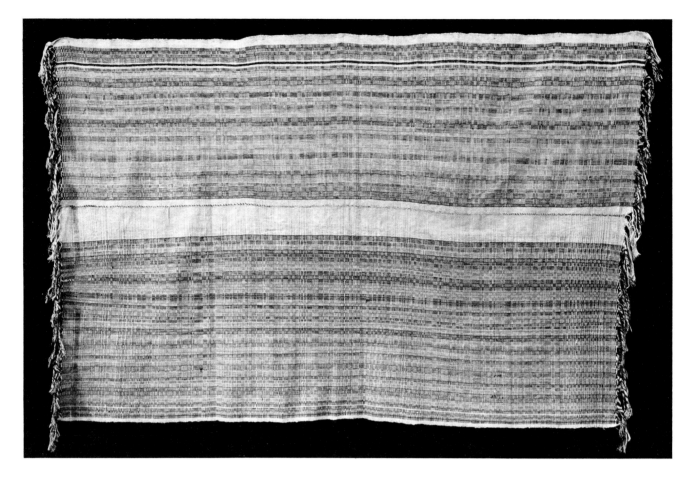

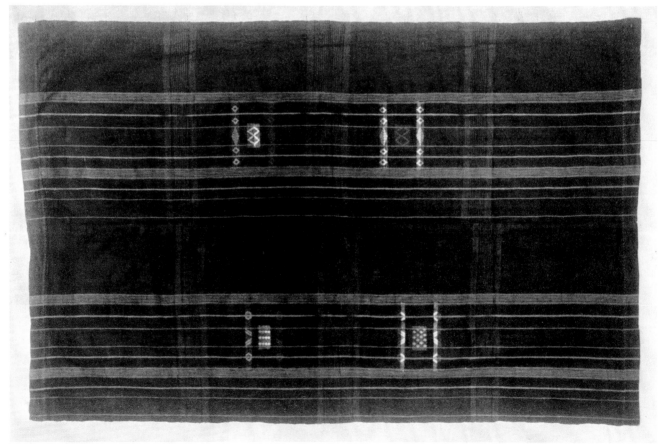

teenth century, Benin cloth was carried by Europeans as a major trade item: "...the striped ones, we sell...on the Gold Coast, where they are in demand; but the entirely blue ones are mostly in demand on the Gabon and Angola."[89]

Nearly all early cloths are described as striped and predominantly blue, a color produced with local dyes, most probably indigo.

The technical aspects of men's weaving on the horizontal loom, such as warp striping, plaiding, weft striping, and brocading, are very much the same as those discussed for women's weaving. However, because edge-sewing is used to make larger swatches of cloth, the result is quite different. A solid color, of course, is essentially unaffected by the edge-sewing process. Similarly, a warp stripe (with monochromatic weft) is unaffected and produces a wide striped cloth (page 195). Since matching is unnecessary, any edge placement results in the same pattern.

However, when even a simple weft stripe is introduced, either the edges may be matched to produce a stripe at right angles to the warp (page 184), or the stripes may be alternated, yielding a checkerboard pattern (page 185). Moreover, matches and misses may be arranged to create a play on stripes and checkerboards (pages 186, 187). Stripes or bands usually cross the entire width of the cloth and can be far more complicated than a simple symmetrical alternation of ABABA, as for example in a design of ABCDEDCBA, where each letter is a stripe of distinct design. In the resulting cloth, half the length (warp) of the cloth will be a mirror image of the other half. The Jukun cloth (page 188) is an excellent example of a particularly complicated design of this sort. The so-called Hausa blanket (page 189) and the tent-hanging from Niger (page 190) are variations on the same theme and share some of the geometric motifs that are widespread in the western Sudan.

Whereas careful measurement, precise calculations, and meticulous thread counts can create a scheme of fixed or repeated patterns, less planning may result in quite dramatic, random designs. Actually, the accidentals in such cloths are not unanticipated, but are allowed for if not calculated. Indeed, in the Yatenga blanket (page 191, top) the carefully controlled stripes and matches make the haphazard juxtapositions of the smaller colored forms all the more exciting. The Upper Volta cloth (page 191, bottom) and the Bonwire *kente* (page 192) carry the technique of the random to brilliant if quite startling ends.

The addition of brocade heddles to the horizontal loom allows the overlay of yet another set of forms upon the strip aesthetic

(continued on page 196)

182

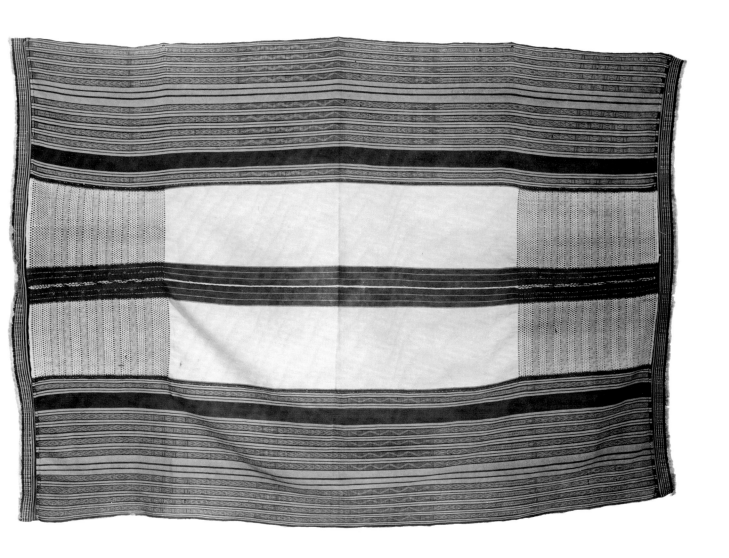

opposite WOMEN'S WEAVE. Fulani, Nigeria. 53
x 31 in. Collection David W. Ames, Mill Valley,
California. Collected in 1964.

above MEN'S WEAVE. Origin unknown. 54 x 45
in. The Museum of the Philadelphia Civic Center. The striped pattern containing small loz-
enge-shaped motifs seems related to old traditional patterns found along the coast from
Senegal to Portuguese Guinea.

183

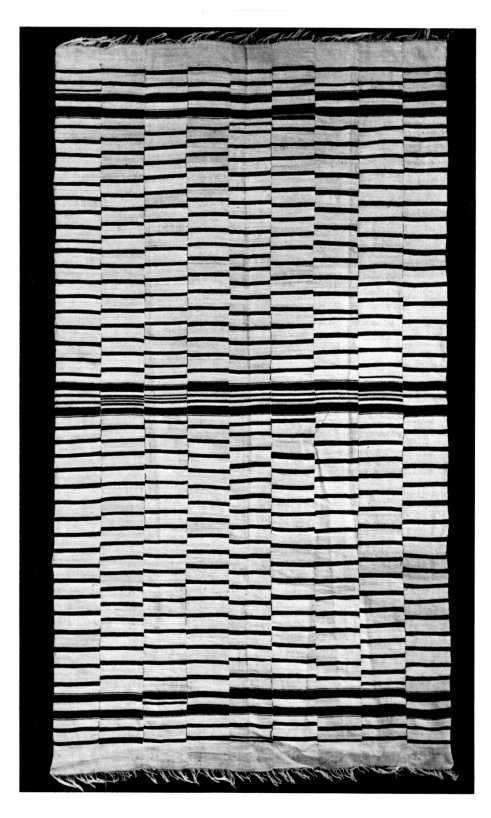

MEN'S WEAVE. Upper Volta. 87 x 54 in. Private collection. A strip weave with black weft stripes, edge-sewn to produce a pattern at right angles to the length (warp) of the cloth.

MEN'S WEAVE. Bambara, Mali. 87 x 50 in. Private collection. A strip weave with black weft stripes, here alternated when sewn together to create a checkerboard pattern.

MEN'S WEAVE. Niger. 104 x 60 in. Field Museum of Natural History, Chicago. Collected in 1968 by Susan Vogel. A black-and-white cloth with touches of red.

MEN'S WEAVE. Mandingo, Guinea. 96 x 66 in. The American Museum of Natural History, New York. This cloth, like the one on the page opposite, exhibits a more complicated mixing of stripe and checkerboard patterns. The concept of an endless strip (see page 195) is replaced by one of units, each unit being equal to the length of the finished cloth.

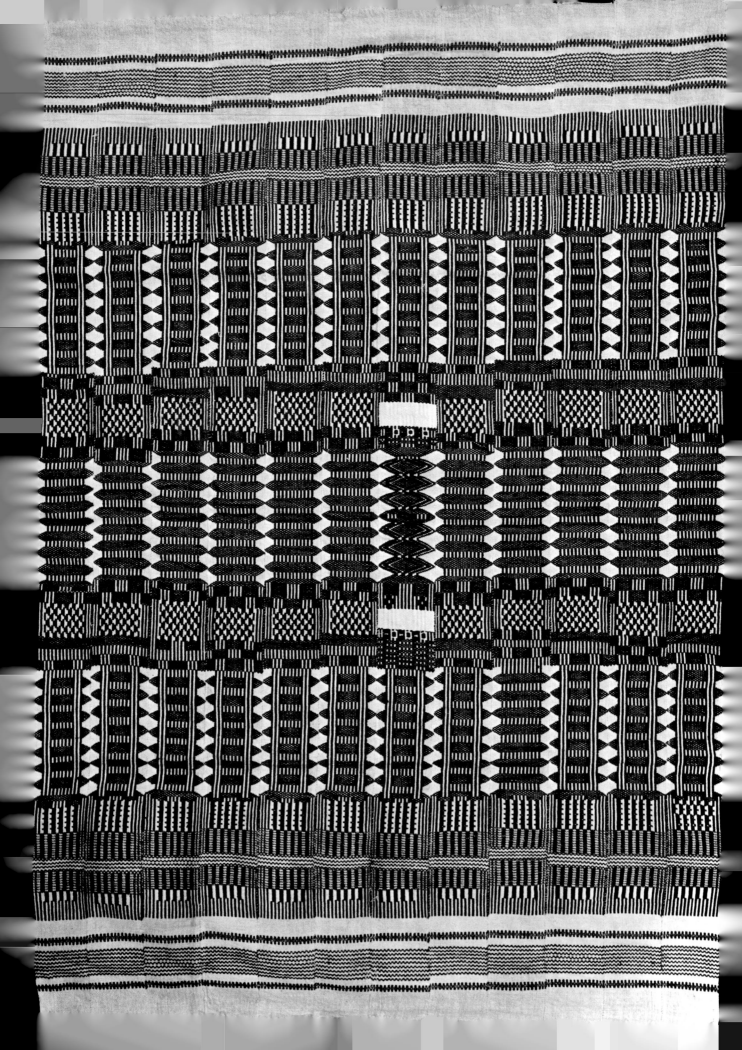

opposite MEN'S WEAVE. Jukun, Nigeria. 65 x
46 in. Collection Dr. and Mrs. Arnold Rubin,
West Los Angeles. Collected in Wukari in 1965.
In this cloth and the two that follow, quite
complicated matching is required to produce a
symmetrical pattern of stripes; one half of the
warp length is a mirror image of the other half.

right MEN'S WEAVE. Origin uncertain. 132 x 60
in. Collection Dr. and Mrs. René A. Bravmann,
Seattle. Collected in Ghana in 1967. A woolen
textile, variously called a Hausa, Timbuctu, or
camel blanket. The colors are black and red on
a white background with embroidered dots.

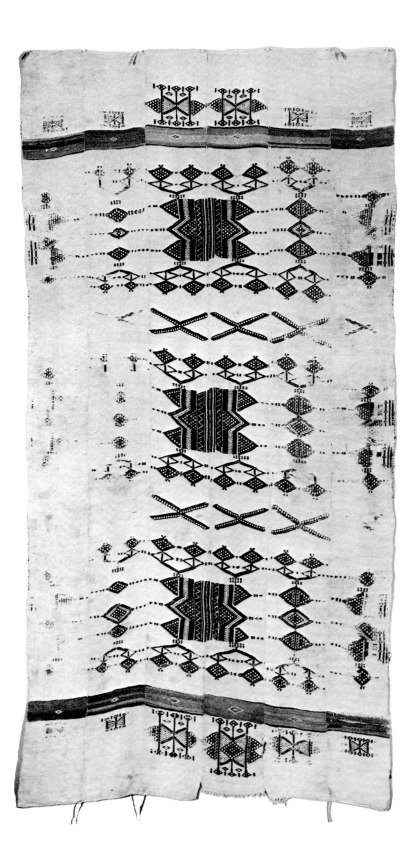

189

above MEN'S WEAVE. Woga, Niger. 166 x 50 in.
Collection Labelle Prussin, Austin, Texas. A
woven, woolen tent-hanging in yellow, white,
and dark brown on a dark red base.

opposite above MEN'S WEAVE. Mossi, Upper
Volta. 108 x 66 in. The American Museum of
Natural History, New York. Collected in Yatenga in 1942. A cloth combining the meticulous matching of weft stripes with an apparently random scattering of small color patterns.
Red, yellow, and black on a white ground.

opposite below MEN'S WEAVE. Upper Volta (?).
87 x 56 in. Private collection. A superb example
of seemingly random placement of pattern.
However, the careful matching of the ends of
the cloth dispels the impression of an uncalcu-
lated overall design.

190

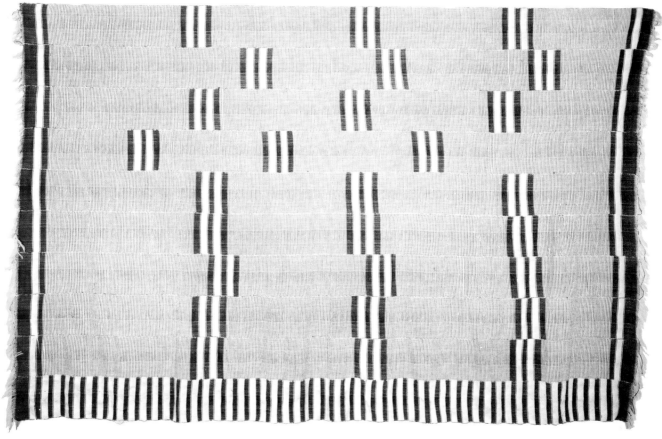

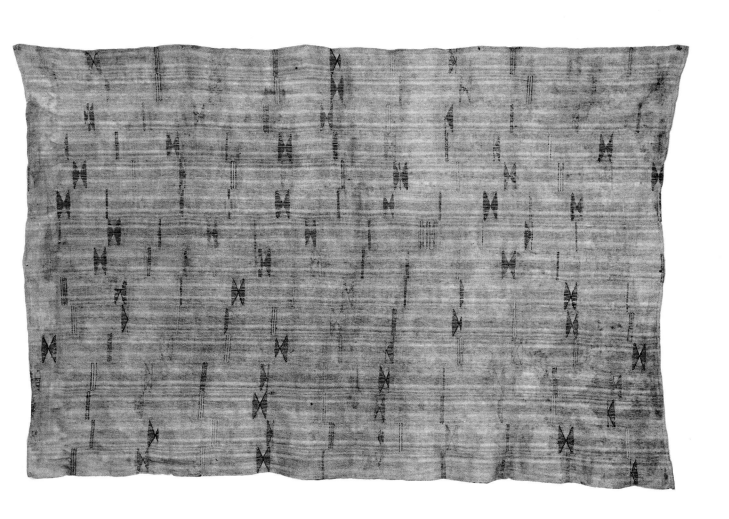

opposite MEN'S WEAVE. Akan/Ashanti, Ghana.
72 x 60 in. UCLA Museum of Cultural History,
Los Angeles. Collected at Bonwire by Labelle
Prussin. A cloth combining fifteen strips, each
of a different pattern, to create a fascinating
priest's robe of black and white cotton.

above MEN'S WEAVE. Liberia (?). 86 x 58 in.
The Museum of the Philadelphia Civic Center.
A strip weave with simple brocade patterns of
added weft threads in black and red.

193

above MEN'S WEAVE. Akan/Ashanti, Ghana. 96 x 60 in. The American Museum of Natural History, New York. *Kente,* a prestige cloth of the Ashanti and related groups, exhibiting brocade and overweave patterns that result from one or more added pairs of heddles.

opposite MEN'S WEAVE. Nigeria. 70 x 44 in. Milwaukee Public Museum. A typical strip weave produced on a man's narrow horizontal loom. The pattern results from sewing together bands of the "endless" warp stripe to create a large cloth.

(page 193). The result in West Africa is the Yoruba *asoke* (pages 202, 203) and the Ghana *kente* (pages 194, 197–200). Traditionally, the wearing of *kente* was the prerogative of Akan royalty who, in 1817, "...wore Ashante cloths, of extravagant price from the costly foreign silks which had been unravelled to weave them in all the varieties of colour, as well as pattern; they were of incredible size and weight and thrown over the shoulder exactly like the Roman toga...."[90]

A quite different effect can be achieved from the matching of shapes that do not completely cross the width of the cloth (page 204). This fitting of forms can result in a dramatic, single, total pattern (page 205), distinct from the repetition of stripe motifs.

It must be emphasized that woven designs are basically controlled or determined by the right-angle crossing of the warp and weft. Thus all the patterns, even the brocade elements, must at least be conceived and executed within a rectangular grid. Embroidery and other decorative elements added to a cloth need not follow this grid—the artisan may or may not choose to emphasize the geometric structure of the cloth. This explains the sharp contrast between the rectangularity of the embroidered patterns on Kasai cloths, reflecting the grid of the raffia mat (page 169), and Hausa embroidery, which tends to ignore it (pages 36, 37). Appliqué (pages 42; 206, bottom), often mixed with embroidery (page 206, top), rarely acknowledges the structure of the basic fabric.

Painting clearly has no reason to follow warp and weft patterns. Yet, both a Senufo painted costume (page 207, top) and a Bambara hunter's cloth (page 209) seem to carry an echo of the striping of woven cloths. Another and much more complicated technique of painting occurs among the Bambara. A vocabulary of semi-abstract symbols (page 208), essentially geometric in nature, is used to decorate both men's and women's clothing. A specially prepared mud dye is applied repeatedly to darken the background; the patterns thus appear in yellowish-white on a dark-brown base.[91]

As noted earlier, beaten bark cloth may be painted (page 157). At times stamped designs appear on locally woven (page 30) or imported cotton. The best-known stamped cloths of West Africa are the *adinkra* cloths of the Ashanti.

The basic technique of indigo dyeing is described in Barbot: "The women and their daughters dress the cotton, then spin and dye it in indigo, for their striped cloths. This colour is extracted from the juicy leaves of a bush they call *Tinto,* somewhat resembling wall-rue. They gather these leaves early in the morning,

(continued on page 201)

MEN'S WEAVE. Ghana. 113 x 83 in. Collection Fred M. Fernald, Alexandria, Virginia. Collected by the owner's uncle, Robert F. Fernald, first American Consul to the Gold Coast. *Kente,* a prestige cloth, was found mainly among Akan groups, but was worn by the Ewe as well. This cloth may be Ewe.

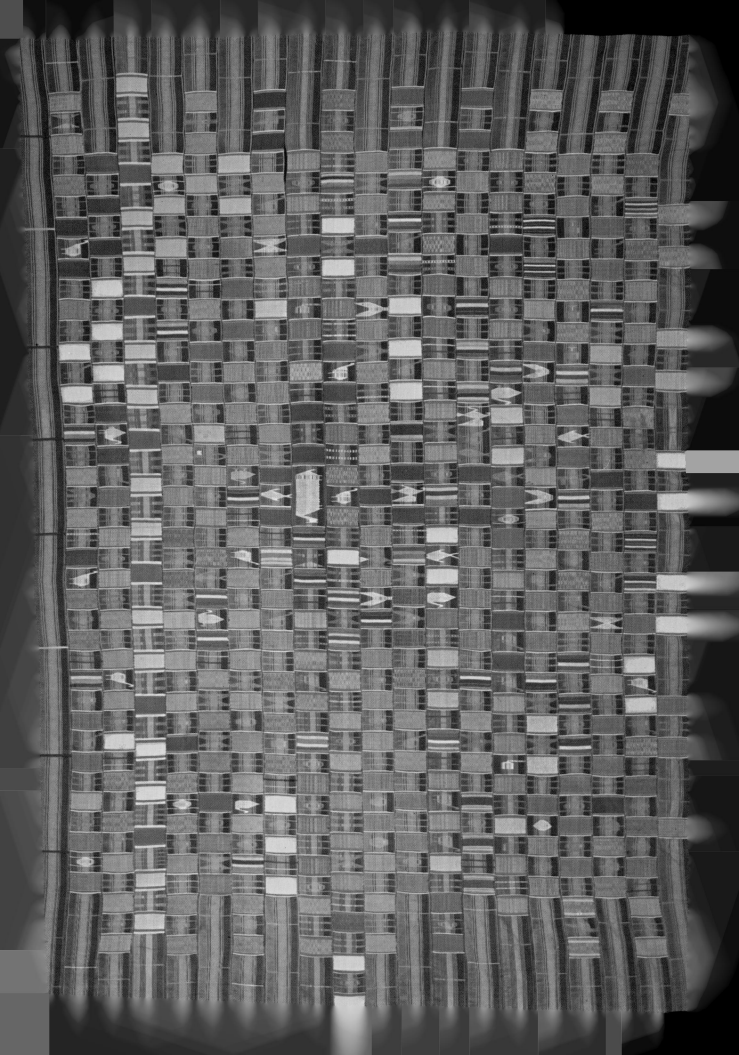

above MEN'S WEAVE. Akan/Ashanti, Ghana.
124 x 32 in. The Brooklyn Museum, New York.
A *kente* cloth.

opposite MEN'S WEAVE *(detail)* Akan/Ashanti,
Ghana. 96 x 48 in. The American Museum of
Natural History, New York. Collected in 1951.
A *kente* cloth of the "Gold Dust" pattern. Both
individual motifs and overall designs of *kente*
have particular names and symbolic meanings.

before the dew of the night falls off, and then bruise or pound them in large deep wooden mortars. When sufficiently beaten, they make rolls or balls of the mass so bruised together, as big as their fists and expose them to the sun for some days to dry. Then they pound it again, and put it into a pot, which has a hole in the bottom, and is fill'd up with a quantity of ashes made of the wood of the same tree, and this set within another pot. Then for some time they pour clear spring water over the ashes, which by degrees penetrates quite through into the under pot; and this being repeated, as often as is thought requisite, they set the under pot for ten days in the sun, which thickens the liquor in it, like cream, the top whereof they take off gently, and with it dye as with indigo. The gross matter that remains in the pot, they throw away."[92]

This description matches remarkably closely the technique used today in Nigeria.[93] Another report from 1785 for the Akreen seems identical.[94] Although there are reports of other colors —black, yellow, and red in particular—indigo seems to have been the most common and most popular.

Resist dyeing, really a series of methods or devices to protect parts of a cloth while allowing others to receive a dye, results in quite spectacular cloths that are extremely popular in West Africa. No references to resist dyeing have been noted in early travelers' reports, and there is no certainty about its origins or early distribution. However, present-day raffia tie dyeing (pages 207, bottom; 210) may hint at long tradition.

The most common methods of resist dyeing are tie and dye, sew and dye, and the use of a paste resist. In tie dyeing, the cloth can be self-tied. If a single knot is dyed, the result is a large area that has resisted the dye (page 211). To create more intricate patterns, smaller knots may be tied with cotton or raffia strings (page 218), or the cloth may be folded or crumpled and tied (page 219) before dyeing. Designs may be sewed on the cloth and the stitches later picked out after dyeing to reveal a light-on-dark pattern.

Resist dyeing using cassava paste is similar to batik, inasmuch as a substance that will resist the penetration of the dye is arranged in a pattern on the cloth. It may be painted directly on the cloth (pages 224, 225), or it may be applied through a stencil (page 217). The result as found among the Yoruba is an extremely popular cloth called *adire,* which is made in a large number of patterns, each with its own name. New designs are continually being invented as older motifs go out of fashion.

The resistant compound, which sometimes is a wax rather than cassava paste, may be applied with stamps, as in a group of related cloths from the Ivory Coast (pages 220–223).

(continued on page 216)

MEN'S WEAVE *(detail).* Akan, Ghana (?). 95 x 32 in. Collection Jack Lenor Larsen, New York. A brilliant textile, unusual for either Ghana or Nigeria. It closely resembles *kente,* although the asymmetrical striping of the narrow strips is quite unexpected.

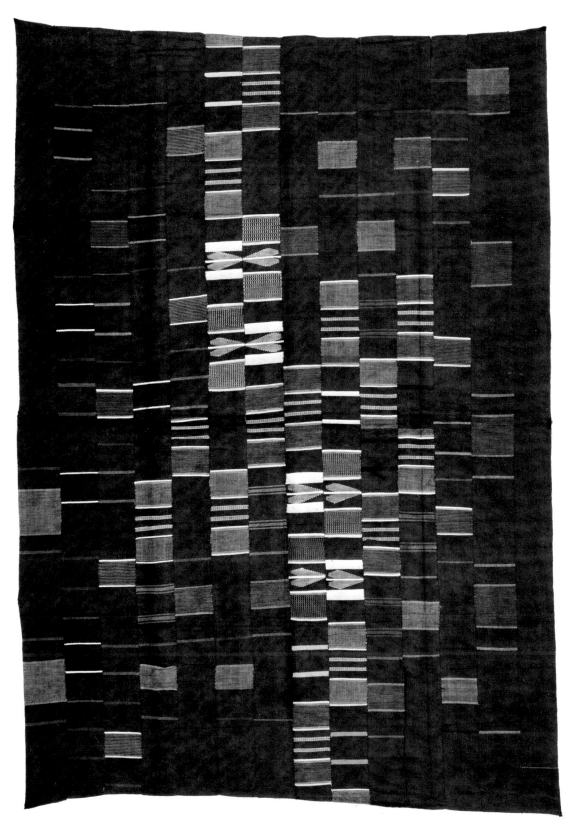

MEN'S WEAVE *(detail opposite)*. Yoruba, Oyo,
Nigeria. 84 x 60 in. The American Museum of
Natural History, New York. Collected in 1948.
A complicated brocade pattern of supplement-
ary weft threads.

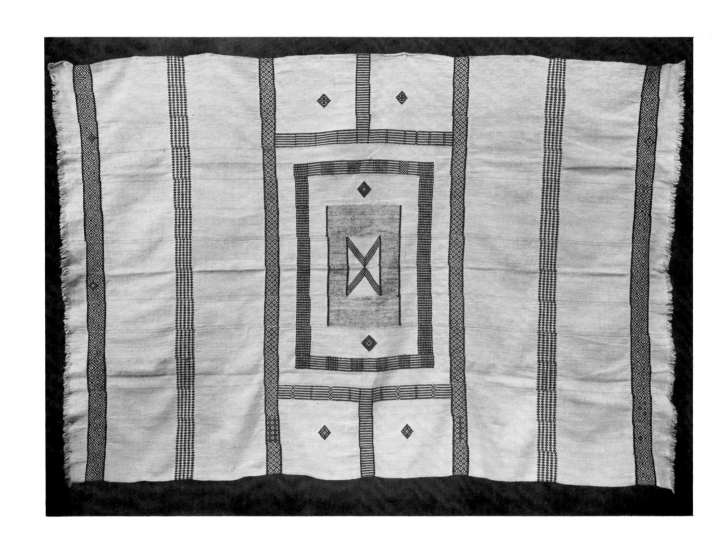

above MEN'S WEAVE. Origin uncertain. 86 x 56 in. Private collection. The large central design of this textile introduces yet a different concept of strip weaving. In place of a repeated pattern, the cloth is conceived as a single unit. Thus each strip is calculated so as to produce a design having mirror symmetry both horizontally and vertically.

opposite MEN'S WEAVE. Liberia. 100 x 65 in. Collection Mr. and Mrs. Robert Nooter, Washington, D.C. A large textile functioning as a single design unit, the antithesis of the simple edge-sewn, warp-stripe cloth.

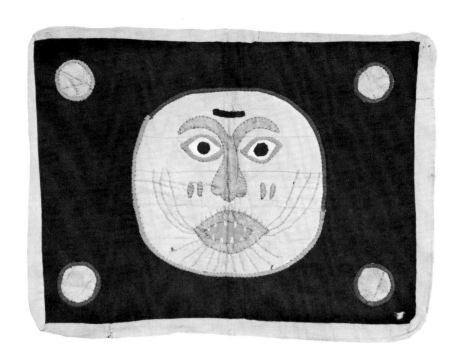

above APPLIQUED PILLOW COVER. Fon, Dahomey. 17 x 13 in. The Herskovits Collection,
Evanston, Illinois. Appliquéd and embroidered
prestige cloth depicting the sun.

below APPLIQUED GOWN. Akan, Ghana. 75 x
47 in. Private collection. A chiefly tunic of appliquéd felt designs, said to have belonged to
Kofi Kamami of Jamasi.

above PAINTED COSTUME. Senufo, Ivory Coast. L. ca. 50 in. Collection Henri A. Kamer, New York. Probably intended to be worn with a horizontal mask.

below RAFFIA SKIRT. Ngala, Republic of Zaïre. 31 x 14 in. The Peabody Museum of Salem, Massachusetts. Collected before 1892. One of the simplest sorts of tie dyeing.

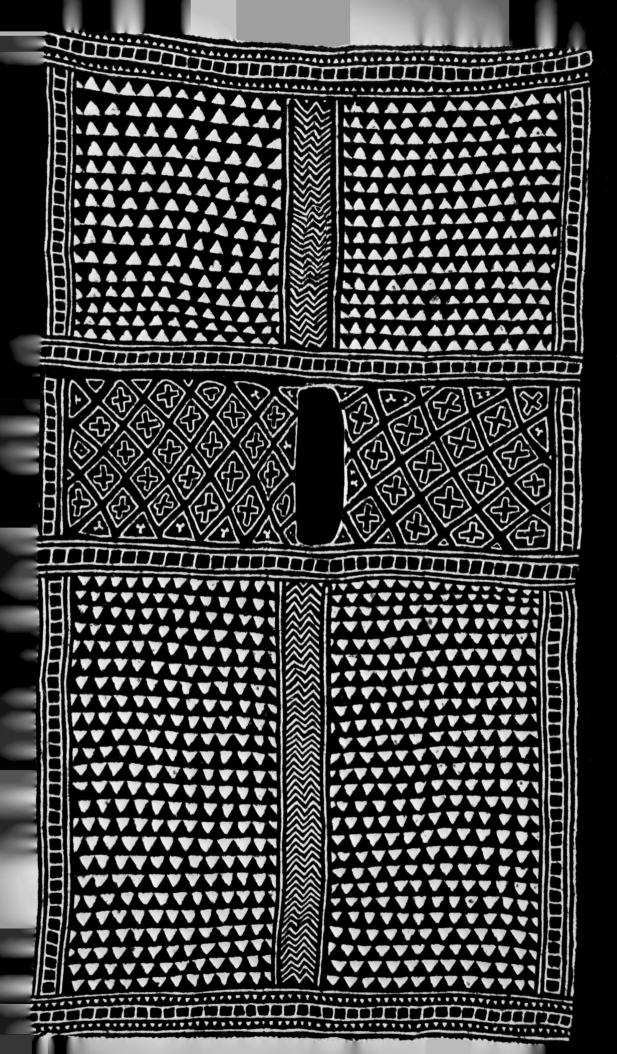

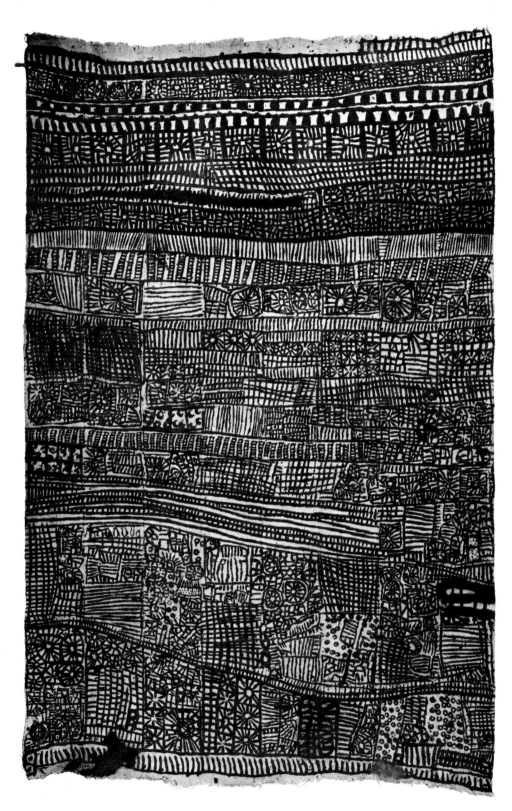

opposite PAINTED SHIRT. Bambara, Mali. 56 x 32 in. Collection Katherine White Reswick, Los Angeles. Called by the Bambara *Bokolanfini* (mud cloth).

above PAINTED CLOTH. Bambara, Mali. 67 x 43 in. Collection Charles and Joan Bird, Bloomington, Indiana. Collected in Kolokani, the center for production of Bambara hunters' painted cloths.

TIED-AND-DYED RAFFIA SKIRT. Dida, Ivory Coast. L. 36 in. Collection Mrs. Genevieve McMillan, Cambridge, Massachusetts. A tubular skirt of plaited (?) raffia fiber. It has been dyed twice.

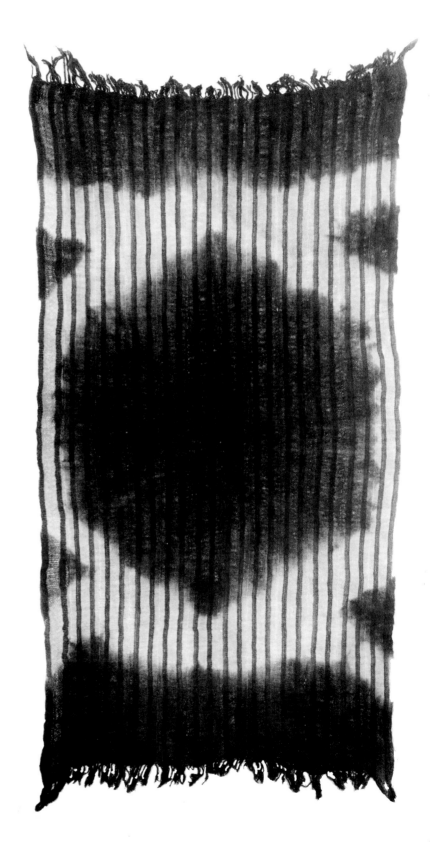

TIED-AND-DYED CLOTH. Tiv, Nigeria. 52½ x
29 in. The African Collections, Lincoln University, Pennsylvania. Collected in 1912. A cloth of
fine gauze strips with a warp stripe has been
tied into a single large knot and dyed with
indigo.

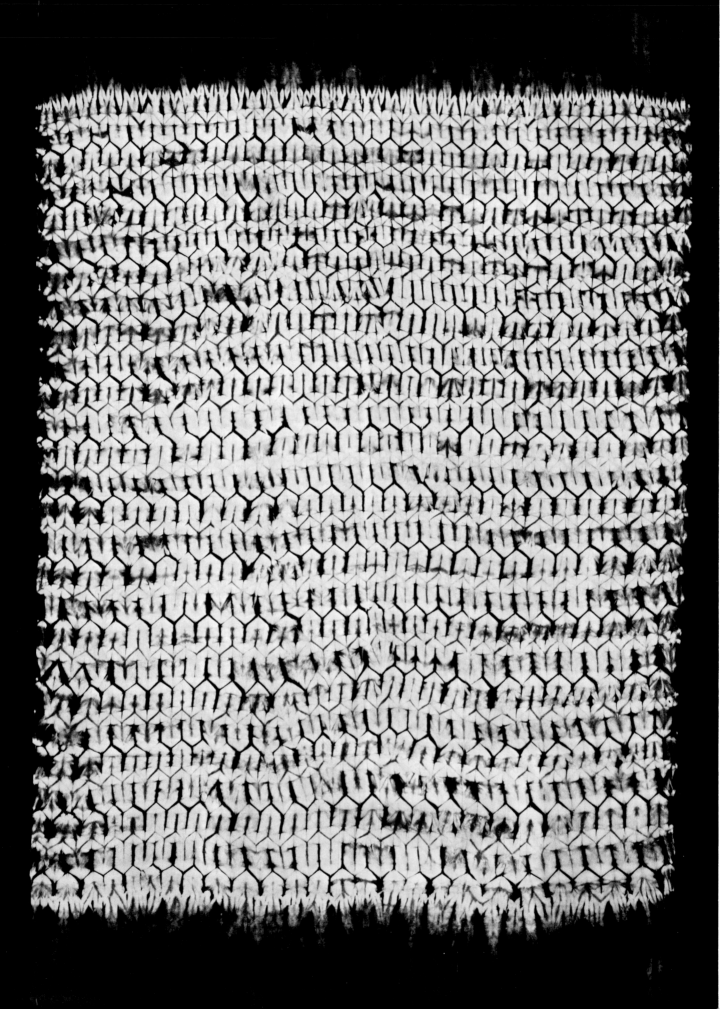

opposite TIED-AND-DYED CLOTH. Mende, Sierra Leone. 64 x 42 in. Collection Mrs. Clare K. Gebauer, McMinnville, Oregon. Collected in 1969.

above TIED-AND-DYED CLOTH. Dioula, Ivory Coast. 62 x 38 in. Field Museum of Natural History, Chicago. Collected in 1968 in Lolobo by Susan Vogel. A strip weave that has been tied and dyed over woven stripes.

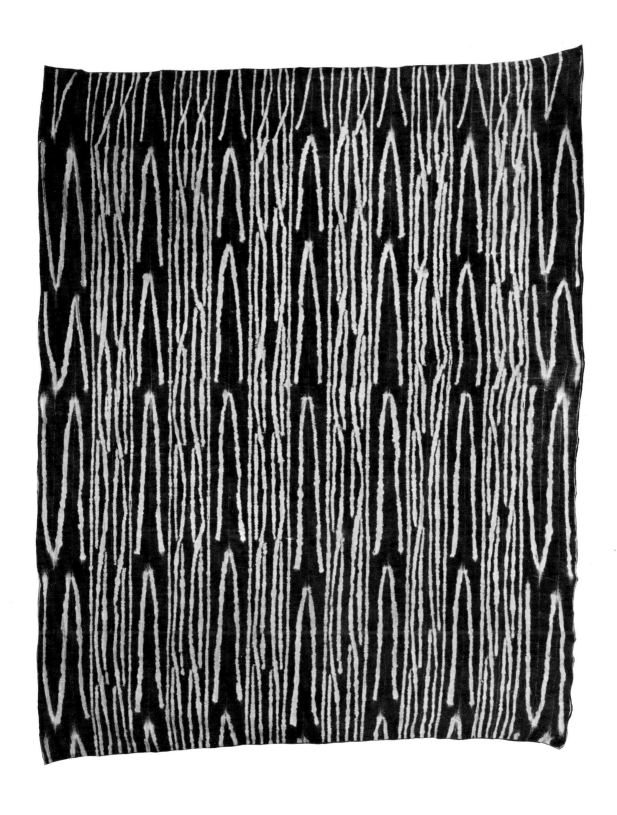

opposite TIED-AND-DYED CLOTH. Ghana. 91 x 64 in. The Peabody Museum of Salem, Massachusetts. Collected before 1927.

above PAINTED-RESIST-DYED CLOTH. Bamum, Cameroon. 87 x 66 in. Private collection. A cloth in the python design.

215

HAVING LOOKED, however briefly, at African arts of personal adornment, it is apparent that each craft has its own history and aesthetic. Each is also a lively art, carrying traditional techniques and motifs into modern uses. To attempt to describe the nature of African dress one must consider a multitude of distinct styles, forms, and fashions. The size and ethnic diversity of the subcontinent would seem to make that task difficult if not impossible.

Despite this complexity some broad patterns do emerge. The untailored wraparound garment, for example, has existed for centuries. Tailoring techniques seem to be an overlay on this base, with European dress an even later addition. Further, the appearance of tailoring seems related to that of the horizontal strip loom, both possibly having been brought to West Africa along the old trans-Saharan trade routes.

Thus a map showing ancient modes of costume would show a very wide distribution not only of wraparound, untailored dress, but of techniques and materials such as beaten bark cloth, woven or plaited raffia and bast, and leatherworking. Techniques of painting or dyeing with camwood and indigo would also seem to be old industries that did not depend on imported materials or techniques.

Such a map might also show the later, outside influences, which moved across the Sahara, up the Nile, and into east Africa, most probably following the routes established by traders in search of gold, ivory, or slaves. Metalworking techniques, especially lost-wax casting, very likely followed the same routes, for wherever gold, silver, or copper alloys are worked into jewelry, historical contact with the Mediterranean Coast or the Indian Ocean trade can be demonstrated.

If carried into the present, this imaginary map would show two additional layers: styles of dress and fashion adopted from the Europeans in the modern period; and styles of dress adopted from traditional forms in a time of increasing national identity.

It is hoped that the works illustrated here and their accompanying comments have served to introduce the reader to the richness and diversity of the African arts of personal adornment, and that they may encourage further exploration of a little-known and underappreciated body of artistic achievement. Until intensive investigations based on rigorous methodologies have been carried out, we must continue to await the formulation of the clear definitions and analyses that are eventually to be hoped for in this area of world art.

STENCILED-RESIST-DYED CLOTH. Yoruba, Abeokuta, Nigeria. 75 x 32 in. Collection Mr. and Mrs. Sylvester Obi Akalonu, Los Angeles. Collected in 1964. A European printed cloth on which a design is applied by forcing cassava paste through a zinc stencil before dyeing. A type of *adire* cloth.

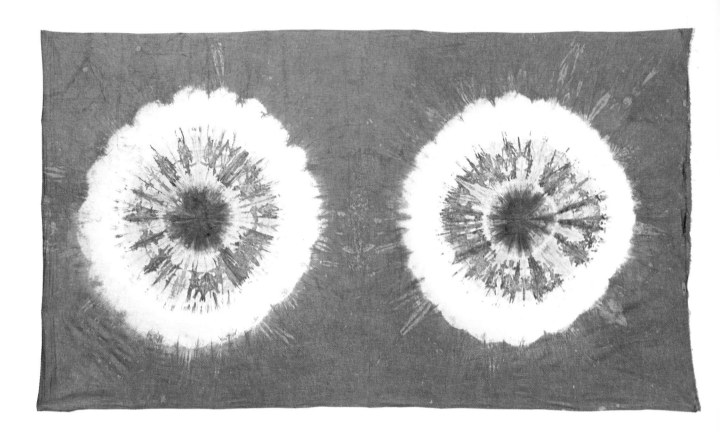

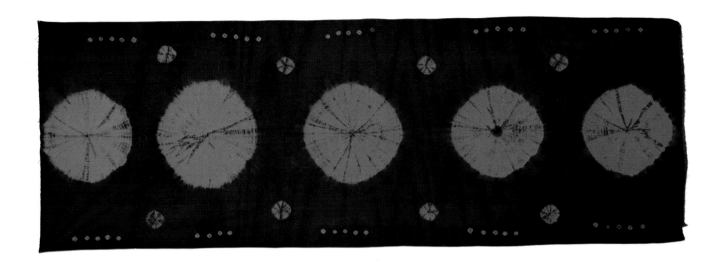

above TIED-AND-DYED CLOTH. Senegal. 112 x 32 in. Collection Dr. and Mrs. Roy Sieber, Bloomington, Indiana. Collected in 1967. A cloth that has been dyed twice—with indigo and kola on white imported cloth.

below TIED-AND-DYED CLOTH. Yoruba, Abeokuta, Nigeria. 95 x 36 in. Collection Kay L. McGlachlin, Los Angeles. An *adire* cloth, dyed with indigo over a red imported fabric.

opposite TIED-AND-DYED CLOTH. Dioula, Upper Volta. 64 x 45 in. Private collection. Combines folding and crumpling techniques.

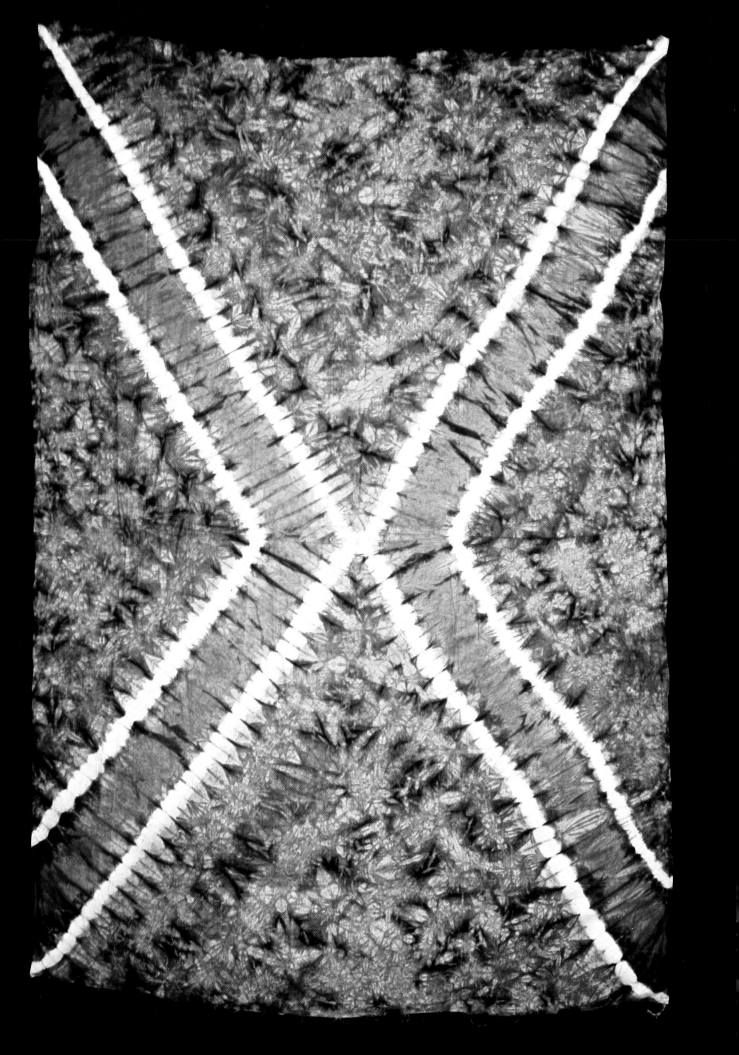

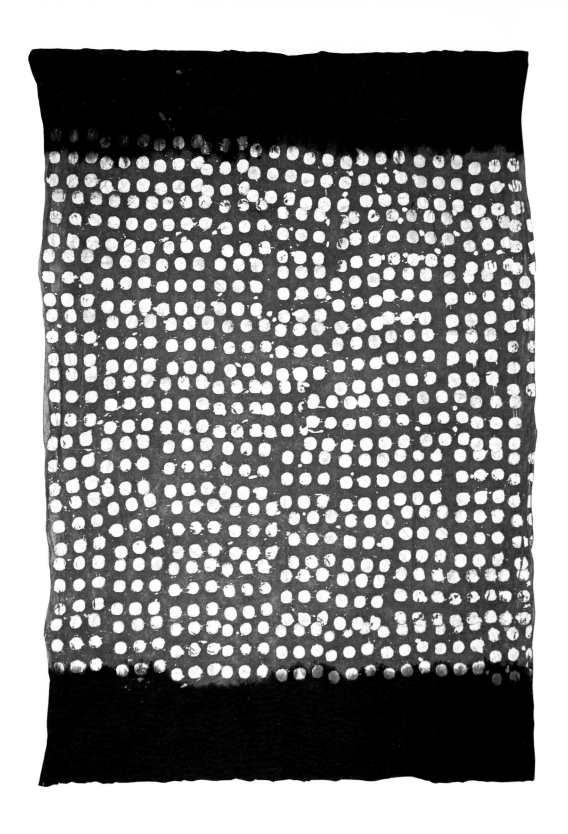

GROUP OF RESIST PRINTS. Ivory Coast. Average size 67 x 47 in. Private collection. The cloths that appear on pages 220–223 have been stamped with the resistant material, cassava paste or possibly wax, before dyeing. They demonstrate the continued vitality of the decorative arts in modern Africa.

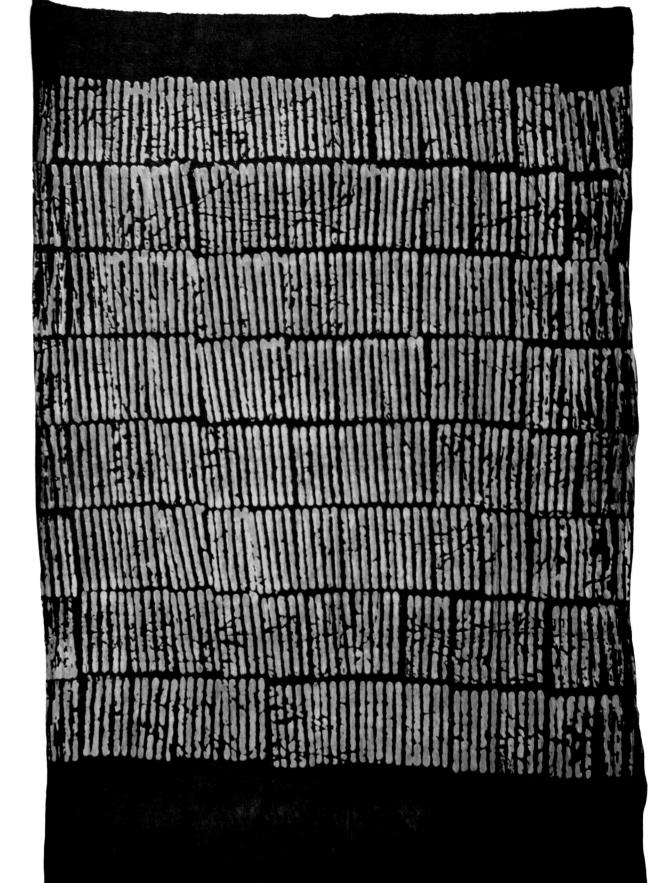

left MADAME SARIYU ABEJE of Ede, Nigeria, painting on cloth with cassava-paste resist, the first step in producing a Yoruba *adire,* resist-dyed cloth.

opposite PAINTED-RESIST-DYED CLOTH. Yoruba, Nigeria. 78 x 66 in. Collection Mr. and Mrs. Jo Dendel, Costa Mesa, California. Collected in 1941. One of the traditional cassava-paste-painted resist cloths. This design is called *olokun.*

NOTES

1. John Barbot, *A Description of the Coasts of North- and South-Guinea* . . . (London: 1732), p. 237.

2. Marchais, quoted in Thomas Astley, *A New General Collection of Voyages and Travels* . . . (London: 1745–1747), vol. 3, p. 43.

3. Barbot, *op.cit.,* p. 143.

4. *Ibid.,* pp. 143 and 131.

5. Comment offered at Columbia Seminar on Primitive Art, Columbia University, New York, March 24, 1972.

6. James Barbot, Jr., in Astley, *op.cit.,* vol. 3, p. 208.

7. Peggy Harper, "The Role of Dance in the Gelede Ceremonies of the Village of Ijio," *Odu,* New Series, no. 4 (October, 1970), p. 70. Miss Harper's notes offer interesting possibilities for analysis of the relationship between daily action patterns and dance movements.

8. Astley, *op.cit.,* vol. 3, p. 119.

9. John Barbot, *op.cit.,* p. 239.

10. From "The Voyage of Cado Mosto," in John Hamilton Moore, *A New and Complete Collection of Voyages and Travels* (London: 1785?), vol. 1, pp. 433–434. Cf. Astley, *op.cit.,* vol. 1, p. 582.

11. Barbot, *op.cit.,* p. 35. This mention of plaiting may be the earliest reference to embroidery in African costume.

12. Quoted in J. H. Moore, *op.cit.,* vol. 1, p. 318.

13. Barbot, *op.cit.,* p. 35.

14. Astley, *op.cit.,* vol. 3, p. 54.

15. Barbot, *op.cit.,* p. 237. An ell = 45 inches.

16. *Ibid.,* p. 238.

17. *Ibid.,* p. 239.

18. This and the following passages are based on Paul Erdman Isert, *Voyages en Guinée et dans les îles Caraïbes* (1793), pp. 162 ff. This book is composed of letters, most of them written in 1785.

19. Barbot, *op.cit.,* p. 347, in a description of Ardra.

20. An important film, *Benin Kingship Rituals,* by Francis Speed and W. Bradbury, could serve as a basis for an analysis of the courtly costumes.

21. Astley, *op.cit.,* vol. 3, p. 251.

22. Peter Kolben's voyage in *The World Displayed; or A Curious Collection of Voyages and Travels* (London: 1759), vol. 1, pp. 59–60.

23. *Ibid.,* p. 61.

24. Thomas E. Bowdich, *Mission From Cape Coast Castle to Ashantee,* 3rd ed. (New York: Barnes and Noble, 1966), p. 37. First published in London in 1819.

25. Michel Leiris and Jacqueline Delange, *African Art,* translated from the French by Michael Ross (New York: Golden Press, 1968), Pl. 160.

26. Barbot, *op.cit.,* pp. 59–62.

27. *Ibid.,* p. 62.

28. *Ibid.,* p. 129. The reference is to the Rio Sestro area of Liberia.

29. *Ibid.,* p. 237. The reference is to the area of modern-day Ghana.

30. *Ibid.,* p. 295.

31. Marchais, quoted in Astley, *op.cit.,* vol. 3, p. 43.

32. John Harris, *Navigantium atque itenerantium bibliotheca, or a Complete Collection of Voyages* . . . (London: 1744), vol. 1, p. 803.

33. See Robert F. Thompson's fine essay, "The Sign of the Divine King," *African Arts,* vol. 3, no. 3 (Spring 1970), pp. 2–17, 74–80.

34. G. Schwab, *Tribes of the Liberian Hinterland,* George W. Harley, ed., Peabody Museum, Harvard University, Cambridge, Mass., 1947; Kraus Reprint, 1968, Fig. 82a.

35. File E6756 in Archives of the Peabody Museum of Salem, Massachusetts.

36. Based on observations made particularly in northern Ghana.

37. Sieur d'Elbée, describing Prince Tozifon of Ardra in 1670, in J. H. Moore, *op.cit.*, vol. 1, p. 142.

38. Entry no. 141 in museum catalogue *Masterpieces from the Sir Henry Wellcome Collection at UCLA* (Los Angeles: UCLA Museum of Cultural History 1966).

39. Bowdich, *op.cit.*, p. 39.

40. Quoted in Sara Lane, "African Weapons and Tools," *Southern Workman*, vol. 58, no. 8 (1929), p. 354. This sword, now at the Hampton Institute, quite probably is the one depicted in the famous king statues of the Kuba.

41. Sieur d'Elbée, quoted in Astley, *op.cit.*, vol. 3, p. 67.

42. Astley, *op.cit.*, vol. 3, p. 5.

43. Barbot, *op.cit.*, pp. 235 and 238.

44. See Emil Torday, "Note on an Unusual Form of Tatu," *Man,* vol. 13 (1913), 2, p. 3.

45. Paul Bohannon, "Beauty and Scarification amongst the Tiv," *Man,* vol. 56 (September 1956), 129, p. 121.

46. Cado Mosto's Second Voyage, 1456, in Astley, *op.cit.*, vol. 1, p. 594.

47. Quoted in J. H. Moore, *op.cit.*, vol. 1, p. 316.

48. In *ibid.*, p. 318.

49. Astley, *op.cit.*, vol. 3, p. 36.

50. Barbot, *op.cit.*, p. 238.

51. I have observed scars resulting from burns on the chest among the Igala of Nigeria; these invariably occurred as part of a curing process, usually during childhood.

52. I am indebted to James Brink for allowing me to use his unpublished manuscript, "The Anthropology and Aesthetics of Body Sculpture in Sub-Saharan Africa," in preparing these notes.

53. See also Herbert M. Cole, *African Arts of Transformation* (Santa Barbara: University of California, 1970).

54. Barbot, *op.cit.*, p. 392. The people lived in the Gabon River area.

55. Cole, *op.cit.*, pp. 17 and 15.

56. Astley, *op.cit.*, vol. 3, p. 216. The reference would seem to date from the sixteenth century and possibly derive from Pigafetta and therefore refer to the Congo area.

57. Barbot, *op.cit.*, p. 392, describing the peoples of Pongo Island in the area of the Gabon River.

58. *Ibid.*, p. 295. The area is modern-day Ghana.

59. Quoted in J. H. Moore, *op.cit.*, p. 434. Cado Mosto's report dates from 1455.

60. Barbot, *op.cit.*, p. 35, referring to Senegal.

61. *Ibid.*

62. Francis Moore, *Travels into the Inland Parts of Africa . . .* (London: Edward Cave, 1738), p. 75.

63. In Astley, *op.cit.*, vol. 3, p. 96.

64. Indeed, the early names for areas of the coast reflected European commercial interests: "Malegueta" or "Grain Coast" (pepper; modern Sierra Leone and Liberia); "Tooth Coast" (ivory; the Ivory Coast); "Gold Coast" (modern Ghana); and, somewhat later, "Slave Coast" (modern Togo, Dahomey, and Nigeria) These designations are general and appear, for example, in Barbot. See also the map (frontispiece) of William Snelgrave, *A New Account of Some Parts of Guinea, and the Slave-Trade* (London: 1734).

65. Personal communication, 1958, from Bernard Fagg, then director of the Department of Antiquities of the Nigerian government and the discoverer of the Nok culture.

66. Astley, *op.cit.*, vol. 3, p. 125.

67. Barbot, *op.cit.*, p. 262.

68. Thurstan Shaw, *Igbo-Ukwu: An Account of Archaeological Discoveries in Eastern Nigeria* (London: Faber and Faber, 1970), vol. 1, pp. 240, 242.

69. Graham Connah, "Archaeology in Benin," *Journal of African History,* vol. 13, no. 1 (1972), p. 31.

70. Astley, *op.cit.*, referring to Towerson's voyage of 1555.

71. I saw a great deal of it in western Ghana and in northern Nigeria in 1958, and recorded dance costumes of painted bark cloth among the Igala.

72. H. Ling Roth, *Studies in Primitive Looms,* 3rd ed. (Halifax, England: Bankfield Museum, 1950), pp. 26 ff. No clear dates have been established for the introduction of the different looms. The men's horizontal strip loom may have been introduced with Islamic culture about the eleventh century.

73. Barbot, *op.cit.*, p. 143.

74. Lopez and Pigafetta (1578) in Astley, *op.cit.*, vol. 3, p. 248.

75. Barbot, *op.cit.*, p. 471.

76. See H. J. Braunholtz, *Sir Hans Sloane and Ethnography*, W. Fagg, ed. (London: British Museum, 1970), Pls. 7, 8.

77. These notes derive from Sara Lane, "African Textile Craftsmanship," *The Southern Workman*, vol. 57, no. 7 (1928), pp. 262–265. The description is probably based on notes from Dr. William H. Sheppard.

78. *Ibid.*, p. 263.

79. Some choice examples of Kuba textiles from museums in England are illustrated in Margaret Trowell, *African Design*, 2nd ed. (New York: Praeger, 1966), Pls. XIX–XXI, XXIV.

80. William H. Sheppard, "African Handicrafts and Superstitions," *The Southern Workman*, vol. 50, no. 9 (1921), pp. 407–408.

81. In Emil Torday and T. A. Joyce, "Notes ethnographiques sur les peuples communément appelés Bakuba . . . ," *Annales du Musée du Congo Belge,* series 3, vol. 2, fasc. 1 (Brussels: 1910). Trowell, *op.cit.*, p. 30, offers a summary.

82. See Jan Vansina, *Kingdoms of the Savanna* (Madison, Milwaukee, and London: University of Wisconsin Press, 1968), p. 120. Other variations occur.

83. In J. H. Moore, *op.cit.*, vol. 1, p. 433. It may also suggest that the weaving was the work of men, for Cado Mosto noted that the men "employ themselves in women's work, such as spinning, washing of cloths, and the like" (p. 434). "The like" might well have included weaving.

84. Barbot, *op.cit.*, pp. 40–41.

85. F. Moore, *op.cit.*, pp. 72–73.

86. *Ibid.*, p. 73.

87. Isert, *op.cit.*, pp. 124–125.

88. Antonio Carreira, *Panaria: Cabo-Verdiano-Guineense Aspectos historicos e socio-economicos* (Lisbon: 1968), *sub* Conclusions.

89. Dapper, reported in H. Ling Roth, *Great Benin* (Halifax, England: F. King & Sons, 1903; reissued London: Routledge and Kegan Paul, 1968), p. 133.

90. Bowdich, *op.cit.*, p. 35.

91. A full description is to be found in Pascal J. Imperato and Maril Shamir, "'Bokolanfini': Mud Cloth of the Bambara of Mali," *African Arts,* vol. 3, no. 4 (Summer 1970), pp. 32–41.

92. Barbot, *op.cit.*, p. 41.

93. This conclusion is based both on my researches at Ede and Ife, and the description in Jane Barbour and Doig Simmons, eds., *Adire Cloth in Nigeria* (Ibadan: University of Ibadan, Institute of African Studies, 1971), especially the section by Nancy Stanfield on dyeing methods.

94. Quoted in Isert, *op.cit.*, p. 125.

SELECTED BIBLIOGRAPHY

This bibliography is arranged in the following categories: General Bibliographies and Culture Surveys; Costume, which encompasses not only wearing apparel but also the arts of body decoration, and includes the observations of early travelers, explorers and missionaries and the writings of ethnographers; Jewelry; and Textiles, with reference to the techniques of manufacture of the latter two.

Until recently the only compilation of books and articles on African costume was contained in L. J. P. Gaskin's *A Bibliography of African Art,* published in 1965 for the International African Institute, London. Organized according to political divisions, Gaskin's book offers a section entitled "Clothing and Adornment" for each country included. Many of the languages represented in the entries are those of the colonial powers that have governed Africa. The book is still a very useful resource for African art studies. For further appreciation of the ethnic groups represented, some general culture surveys are included. In *Africa: Its Peoples and Their Culture History,* by George P. Murdock, major ethnic groups and their language-related families are described in terms of geographic location and social, religious, and economic organization, with a selected bibliography for each group. *Cultures and Societies of Africa,* edited by Simon and Phoebe Ottenberg, is an anthology of papers on such topics as social organization, government, religion, and aesthetics of sub-Saharan peoples. *The African World,* edited by Robert Lystad, and *African Worlds,* edited by C. Daryll Forde, are publications similar in content to the Ottenberg anthology. The *Dictionnaire des civilisations africaines* includes texts by French Africanists, with illustrations in black and white of art styles, objects, and techniques; it contains references to clothing.

For descriptions of costume, the accounts by the first European travelers and explorers present the earliest observations on the apparel of African peoples. Although their primary aim was to discover sources of rivers and set up trade and trade routes, these men were not casual observers of the people they encountered. For example, in Richard Eden's *The Decades of the New World,* 1555, complete and detailed descriptions of the dress and customs of the people he met can be found. Another such account appears in John Atkins' *A Voyage to Guinea, Brazil and the West Indies,* 1737. The contents of the title page are worth quoting, for they are typical of what is included in these publications: "A Voyage . . . in His Majesty's Ships the 'Swallo' and 'Weymouth.' Describing the several Islands and Settlements, vis., Madeira, and the Canaries, Cape de Verde, Sierra Leon, Sesthos, Cape Apollonia, Caba Corso, and others on the Guinea Coast; Barbadoes, Jamaica . . . . in the West-Indies. The Colour, Diet, Languages, Habits, Manners and Religions of the Natives and Inhabitants, with Remarks on the Gold, Ivory and Slave Trade; and on the Winds, Tides and Currents of the several Coasts."

The ethnographies by Frobenius, Torday and Joyce, the Herskovitses, Roth, the Routledges, Ward, and others are later investigations into the economy, habits, and customs of peoples in specific areas. They are generally indexed and illustrated with field photographs and line drawings. Mention is made, specifically or in passing, of the appearance of the natives and of the techniques, such as weaving or matting, employed in transforming raw matter into garments. The

229

ethnographies published by the International African Institute, London, were written by specialists. They contain descriptions of costume, crafts, and their manufacture, but there are no illustrations.

African Dress and *African Textiles* are two very recent compilations on the subject. The former is a "select and annotated bibliography of Subsaharan Countries," by Joanne Bubolz Eicher. It includes 1,025 entries in the English language on all aspects of visual appearance, and is derived from the Gaskin bibliography and the author's own investigation of explorers' and travelers' accounts, missionaries' memoirs, and scholarly and popular materials. The entries also include references to dress or apparel as reflected in plastic works (figural sculpture, masks). Annotation, when it appears, includes page numbers for immediate referral to pertinent materials in the more general sources. *African Textiles* by Cheryl Plumer is an outline of handcrafted textiles. The author presents the history of weaving—including the preparation of yarns, a discussion of looms and weavers, and a listing of the types of textiles and techniques of making them—trade, and a bibliography for each ethnic group represented in the publication. Margaret Trowell's *African Design,* the forerunner of these two later volumes, contains texts and illustrations of designs and techniques of manufacture for walls, mats, screens, textiles, beadwork, and wooden, metal, and ivory objects. In addition she discusses various kinds of body decoration. The book was originally published in 1960 and reissued in two subsequent editions without changes or updating. Therefore, more recent research has made obsolete or corrected some of the author's descriptions of techniques. However, the book is still an important and useful source on this subject. René Gardi's *African Crafts and Craftsmen,* containing numerous color and black and white photographs, describes glassmaking, leatherworking, the dyeing, spinning, and weaving of fabrics, and metalworking in sub-Saharan Africa. Articles on specific techniques can be found in such magazines as *Nigerian Field, Nigeria Magazine,* and *African Arts.*

Roslyn Walker Randall
Department of Afro-American Studies
Indiana University, Bloomington

GENERAL BIBLIOGRAPHIES AND CULTURE SURVEYS

Balandier, Georges, and Jacques Maquet, et al. *Dictionnaire des civilisations africaines.* Paris: Fernand Hazan, 1968.

Forde, C. Daryll. *African Worlds: Studies in the Cosmological Ideals and Social Values of African Peoples.* London, New York, and Toronto: International African Institute, 1959. Reprinted 1968.

Gaskin, L. J. P. *A Bibliography of African Art.* London: International African Institute, 1965.

Gibbs, James L., Jr., ed. *Peoples of Africa.* New York: Holt, Rinehart & Winston, 1965.

Hambly, Wilfrid D. *Source Book for African Anthropology.* Field Museum of Natural History Anthropological Series, vol. 26. Chicago: 1937.

Leiris, Michel, and Jacqueline Delange. *African Art.* Translated by

Michael Ross. New York: Golden Press, 1968.
Chapter 5, "Arts of the Body," on hair-styling, scarification, body painting, textiles, hats, etc.

Leuzinger, Elsy. *Africa: The Art of the Negro Peoples.* New York: Crown, 1967. Original publication, 1960.
Somewhat out of date but contains descriptions of African crafts.

Lystad, Robert, ed. *The African World.* New York: Praeger, 1965.

Murdock, George P. *Africa: Its Peoples and Their Culture History.* New York, Toronto, and London: McGraw-Hill, 1969.

Ottenberg, Simon and Phoebe, eds. *Cultures and Societies of Africa.* New York: Random House, 1960.

COSTUME

Anderson, Efriam. *Contribution à l'ethnographie des Kuta I.* Studia ethnographica upsaliensia, vol. 6. Uppsala: Almqvist & Wiksells, 1953.

Armitage, Cecil Hamilton. *The Tribal Markings and Marks of Adornment of the Natives of the Northern Territories of the Gold Coast Colony.* London: Royal Anthropological Institute, 1924.

Astley, Thomas. *A New General Collection of Voyages and Travels, consisting of the most esteemed relations, which have been hitherto published in many languages: comprehending everything remarkable in its kind, in Europe, Asia, Africa and America.* 4 vols. London: Printed for T. Astley, 1745-1747.

Atkins, John. *A Voyage to Guinea, Brazil and the West Indies . . .* London: 1737.

Barbot, John. *A Description of the Coasts of North- and South-Guinea; and of Ethiopia Inferior, vulgarly Angola, in* Awnsham Churchill. *A Collection of Voyages and Travels, some now first printed from original manuscripts, others now first published in English, . . . With a general preface, giving an account of the progress of navigation, from its first beginning.* London: 1732.
Contains references to cloth and to scarification in Gambia, Senegal River area, Sierra Leone, Ivory Coast, Gold Coast.

Bascom, William R. *The Yoruba of Southwestern Nigeria.* New York: Holt, Rinehart & Winston, 1969.
Description of *egungun* cult and costumes in text and illustrations.

Baxter, P. T. W., and Autrey Butt. *The Azande and Related Peoples of the Anglo-Egyptian Sudan and Belgian Congo.* London: International African Institute, 1953.

Beecham, John. *Ashantee and the Gold Coast.* London: 1841. Reprinted: London: Dawsons of Pall Mall, 1968.

Birnbaum, Martin. "The Long-Headed Mangbetus." *Natural History* (New York), vol. 43, no. 2 (1939), pp. 73–83.

Bowdich, Thomas E. *Mission from Cape Coast Castle to Ashantee, with a Statistical Account of that kingdom and geographical notices of other parts of the Interior of Africa.* London: J. Murray, 1819. Reprinted: New York: Barnes and Noble, 1966.

Bowen, R. L. "The Olu of Itsekiris," *Nigeria Magazine,* no. 22 (1944), pp 62–63. Description of royal crowns.

Bradbury, R. E. *The Benin Kingdom and the Edo-Speaking Peoples of South-Western Nigeria.* London: International African Institute, 1957.

Brain, Robert, and Adam Pollack. *Bangwa Funerary Sculpture.* London: Duckworth, 1971. References to costumes, cloth in Cameroon.

Burrows, Guy. *The Land of Pigmies.* Boston: T. Y. Crowell, 1898.

Burton, Sir Richard F. *Selected Papers on Anthropology, Travel and Exploration.* N. M. Penzer, ed. London: A. M. Philpot, 1924.

Buxton, David. *Travels in Ethiopia.* London: Ernest Benn, 1951.

Cameron, Verney Lovett. *Across Africa.* New York: Harper and Brothers, 1877.

Cerulli, Ernesta. *Peoples of South-West Ethiopia and Its Borderland.* London: International African Institute, 1956.

Cole, Herbert M. *African Arts of Transformation.* Santa Barbara: The Art Galleries, University of California, 1970.
Discussion of dress for ceremonies and rituals, including headpieces and face masks.

Dapper, Olfert. *Description de l'Afrique....* Amsterdam: Wolfgang Waesberge, Boom und Sumerin, 1686. Originally published: *Beschreibung von Africa und einen dazu gehörigen Königreich und Landschaften als Egypten....* Amsterdam: 1668.

Daye, Pierre, Jacques Crokaert, et al. *Le Miroir du Congo Belge.* Brussels and Paris: Aux Editions N. E. A., 1929.
Texts on tattooing, weaving, scarification, metal- and beadworking.

DeGanay, Solange. "On a Form of Cicatrization among the Bambara," *Man,* vol. 49, no. 65 (May 1949), pp. 53–55.

De Negri, Eve. "Hairstyling of Southern Nigeria," *Nigeria Magazine,* no. 65 (June 1960), pp. 191–198.

————."Nigeria's National Dress." *West African Review,* vol. 31, no. 394 (September 1960), pp. 34–39.

————."Yoruba Women's Costumes," *Nigeria Magazine,* no. 72 (March 1962). pp. 4–12.

————."Yoruba Men's Costumes," *Nigeria Magazine,* no. 73 (June 1962), pp. 4–12.

————."Tribal Marks: Decorative Scars and Painting Patterns," *Nigeria Magazine,* no. 81 (June 1964), pp. 106–116.

De Rachewiltz, Boris. *Black Eros: Sexual Customs of Africa from Pre-History to the Present Day.* London: Allen and Unwin, 1964.

Denham, Dixon. *Narrative of Travels and Discoveries in Northern and Central Africa in the Years 1822, 1823, and 1824 by Major Denham, Captain Clapperton, and the late Dr. Oldney.* London: 1826.

Doke, Clement M. *The Lambas of Northern Rhodesia.* London: George G. Harrap, 1931.

Eden, Richard. *The Decades of the New World.* London: 1555.

————.*The History of Trauayle in the West and East Indies, and other countreys lying eyther way, towards the fruitfull and ryche Mulccaes. As Moscovia, Persia, Arabia, Syria, Egypt, Ethiopia, Guinea, China in Cathayo, and Giapan: With a discourse of the Northwest passage ... Gathered in parte, and done into Englyshe by Richarde Eden.* London: 1577.

Eicher, Joanne Bubolz. *African Dress: A Select and Annotated Bibliography of Subsaharan Countries.* East Lansing: Michigan State University, 1969.

Forde, C. Daryll. *Peoples of the Niger-Benue Confluence.* London: International African Institue, 1955.

Freeman, Richard Austin. *Travels and Life in Ashanti and Jaman.* New York: Frederick A. Stokes, 1898.

Frobenius, Leo. *The Voice of Africa.* 2 vols. New York and London: Benjamin Bloom, 1968. First published in 1913.

Gamble, David P. *The Wolof of Senegambia.* London: International African Institute, 1957.

Gardi, René. *African Crafts and Craftsmen.* Translated by Sigrid MacRae. New York, Cincinnati, Toronto, London, and Melbourne: Van Nostrand—Reinhold, 1969.

Germann, Paul. *Die Völkerstämme in Norden von Liberia.* Leipzig: R. Voigtländers, 1933.
Discussion of body painting, hair-styling, weaving.

Goose, D. H. "Tooth Mutilations in West Africans," *Man,* vol. 63 (June 1963), pp. 91–93.

Gorer, Geoffrey. *African Dances.* New York: W. W. Norton, 1962.
References to tattooing, dress; special costumes in photographs.

Grébert, F. *Au Gabon, Afrique équatoriale française.* 3rd ed. Paris: Société des Missions Evangéliques de Paris, 1948.

Grottanelli, Vinigi L. "Somalia Wood Engraving," *African Arts,* vol. 1, no. 3 (Spring 1968), pp. 8–13, 72–73.

"Hairstyles in Angola," *Illustrated London News,* vol. 232 (May 31, 1958), p. 933.

Harley, George W. *Notes on the Poro in Liberia.* Papers of the Peabody Museum of Archaeology and Ethnology, Harvard University, vol. 19, no. 2. Cambridge, Mass: 1941.

Harris, John. *Navigantium atque itinerantium bibliotheca, or A Complete Collection of Voyages and Travels, consisting of above six hundred of the most authentick writers in English, Latin, French, Italian, Spanish, Portuguese, high and low Dutch tongues.* 2 vols. London: T. Woodward, 1744–1748.

Haskins, Sam. *African Image.* New York: Madison Square Press, 1967.
Black and white photographs with author's notes. Costumes in context.

Herskovits, Melville J., and Frances S. *Dahomey: An Ancient West African Kingdom.* 2 vols. New York: J. J. Augustin, 1938. Reprinted: Evanston: Northwestern University Press, 1967.

Hilton-Simpson, M. W. *Land and Peoples of the Kasai.* Chicago: A. C. McClurg, 1912. Reprinted: New York: Negro Universities Press, 1969.

Hobley, Charles W. *Ethnology of A-Kamba and Other East African Tribes.* Cambridge, England: University Press, 1910.
Description of personal ornaments, scarification, tweezers, snuff bottles.

Huntingtonford, G. W. B. *The Galla of Ethiopia: The Kingdoms of Kafa and Janiero.* London: International African Institute, 1955.
Description of hair-styling, ornaments, costumes.

Isert, Paul Erdman. *Voyages en Guinée et dans les îles Caraibes.* 1793.
References to weaving and dyeing along West Guinea coast.

Iyalla, B. S. "Womanhood in the Kalabari," *Nigeria Magazine,* no. 98 (September 1968), pp. 216–224.

Jacoby, Catherine Murray. "Ethiopia Has Its Arts and Cultures," *Arts and Decoration,* vol. 44, no. 4 (November 1935), pp. 12–13.

Jeffreys, M. D. W. "The Bamum Coronation Ceremony as Described by King Njoy," *Africa,* vol. 20 (1950), pp. 38–45.
Description of a special coronation costume.

_____."The Winged Solar Disk or Ibo Itʃi Facial Scarification," *Africa,* vol. 21, no. 2 (April 1951, pp. 93—111.

Johnson, Harry Hamilton, *George Grenfell and the Congo.* 2 vols. London: Hutchinson & Company, 1908.
References to costume, cosmetic techniques, weaving, cloth, etc.

Kingsley, Mary H. *Travels in West Africa: Congo Français, Corisco and Cameroons.* London: 1897. 3rd ed. London: Cass, 1965.

Kyerematen, A. A. Y. *Panoply of Ghana.* London: Longmans, Green, 1964. New York: Praeger, 1964.
Description of royal swords and gold ornaments.

Labat, Jean Baptiste. *Nouvelle relation de l'Afrique occidentale: contenant une description exacte de Sénégal et des pays situés entre le Cap Blanc et la rivière Sierre-Lionne, jusqu'à plus de 300 lieues dans la terre.* Paris: 1728.

_____.*Voyage de Demarchais à Guinée et à Cayene.* Paris: 1730.

Landor, A., and S. Henry. *Across Wildest Africa.* 2 vols. New York: Scribner's, 1907.

Lindblom, Karl Gerkord. *African Razors.* Stockholm: Statens Ethnografiska Museum, 1943.

Little, K. L. *The Mende of Sierra Leone.* London: Routledge and Kegan Paul, 1951.

MacFie, Scott. "A Yoruba Tattooer," *Man,* vol. 13 (1913), pp. 121—122.

MacRow, D. W. "Bamenda Art," *Nigeria Magazine,* no. 57 (1958), pp. 132–153.

Meek, Charles Kingsley. *The Northern Tribes of Nigeria.* 2 vols. London: Oxford University Press, 1925.

_____.*A Sudanese Kingdom.* London: Kegan Paul, 1931. New York: Humanities Press, 1931.
Description of Jukun dress, scarification, etc.

Meyers, Oliver. "A Note on Some Cosmetics Used in Yorubaland," *Odu,* vol. 1, no. 1 (January 1965), pp. 92–103.

Moore, Francis. *Travels into the Inland Parts of Africa: containing a Description of the several Nations for the space of six hundred miles up the River Gambia; their Trade, Habits, Customs, Languages, Manners, Religions, and Government; the power, disposition and characters of some Negro princes; with a particular account of Job Ben Solomon. . . . To which is added, Capt. Stibbs' Voyage up the Gambia in the year 1723 to make Discoveries; with an accurate Map of that River taken on the Spot; and many other Copper-Plates. Also Extracts from the Nubian's Geography (Edrisi's), Leo the African, and other authors ancient and modern, concerning the Niger, Nile and Gambia, and observations thereon. And a Mundingo Vocabulary.* London: Edward Cave, 1738.

Moore, John Hamilton. *A New and Complete Collection of Voyages and Travels.* London: 1785?

Mollien, G. *Travels in the Interior of Africa, to the Sources of*

Senegal and Gambia. T. E. Bowdich, ed. London: 1820. Reprinted: London: Cass, 1967.

Nadel, S. F. *A Black Byzantium: The Kingdom of Nupe in Nigeria.* International Institute of African Languages and Cultures. London: Oxford University Press, 1942.

"National Fashions of Africa," *Ebony* (Chicago), vol. 1, no. 6 (August 1964), pp. 32–138.

Nigeria in Costume. 1st ed. Amsterdam and London: L. van Leer, 1960. 2nd ed. London: Shell Company of Nigeria, 1962.

Odita, E. Okechukwu. *Traditional African Art.* Columbus: Ohio State University Press, 1971.
Exhibition catalogue. Sections on weaving, metals, beads.

Ogunba, Oyin. "Crowns and 'Okube' at Idowa," *Nigeria Magazine,* no. 83 (December 1964), pp. 249–261.

Oliver, B. "Beauty in the Bush," *Nigeria Magazine,* no. 67 (December 1960), pp. 247–255.

Pankhurst, Richard. "The Old Time Handicrafts of Ethiopia with a note on Traditional Dress," *Ethiopia Observer,* vol. 8, no. 3 (1964), p. 221.

Panyella, Augusto. *Esquema de etnologia de los Fang Ntumu de la Guinea Española.* Madrid: Institutode Estudios Africanos, 1959.
Fang facial scarification.

Paquec, Viviana. *Les Bambara.* Paris: Presses Universitaires de France, 1954.
Description of weaving, clothing, hair-styling.

Penn, Irving. "Kirdis of Cameroon," *Vogue* (New York) vol. 154, no. 10 (December 1969), pp. 174–181.
Photographic essay, description of costumes.

Rattray, R. S. *Religion and Art in Ashanti.* Oxford: Clarendon Press, 1927. London: Oxford University Press, 1959, 1969.

Rosevear, D. R. "A Method of Ornamenting the Skin," *Nigerian Field,* vol. 55, no. 2 (April 1936), pp. 69–72.

Roth, H. Ling. *Great Benin: Its Customs, Art and Horrors.* Halifax, England: F. King & Sons, 1903. Reprinted: London: Routledge and Kegan Paul, 1968.
References to weaving, looms, hair-styling, ritual clothing.

Routledge, W. Scoresby, and Katherine. *With a Prehistoric People: The Aki Kuyu of British East Africa.* London: 1910. Reprinted: New York: Barnes and Noble, 1968.

Rowe, C. F. "Abdominal Cicatrizations of the Munshi Tribe, Nigeria," *Man,* vol. 28, no. 131 (1928), pp. 179–80.

Schebesta, Paul. *Among the Congo Pygmies.* London: Hutchinson & Company, 1933.

Schweinfurth, Georg. *The Heart of Africa, Three Years' Travels and Adventures in the Unexplored Regions of Central Africa from 1868–1871.* 2 vols. Translated by Ellen E. Frewer. New York: Harper and Brothers, 1874.

———.*Artes Africanae.* Leipzig: FA Brockhaus, 1875.
Notes on the Mangbetu, hair-styling.

The Secret Museum of Mankind. New York: Manhattan House, n.d.
Contains numerous illustrations, probably pirated, of African ethnic groups in costume.

Sieber, Roy. "The Insignia of the Igala Chief of Eteh, Eastern Nigeria," *Man,* vol. 64 (May-June 1965), pp. 80–82.

Simoons, Frederick J. *Northwest Ethiopia.* Madison: University of Wisconsin Press, 1960.

Snelgrave, Capt. William. *A New Account of Some Parts of Guinea and the Slave Trade, containing I. The History of the late Conquest of the Kingdom of Widaw by the King of Dahome. The Author's Journey to the Conqueror's Camp, where he saw several Captives sacrificed, etc. II. The Manner how the Negroes become Slaves. The Numbers of them yearly exported from Guinea to America. The Lawfulness of that Trade. The Mutinies among them on board the Ships where the Author has been, etc. III. A Relation of the Author's being taken by Pirates in 1719, and the many Dangers he underwent.* London: 1734.

Starr, Frederick. *Congo Natives: An Ethnographic Album.* Chicago: Printed for the author at Lakeside Press, 1912.
Scarification, hair-styling, hats, teeth, in former Belgian Congo.

Talbot, P. Amaury. *The Peoples of Southern Nigeria.* 3 vols. London: Oxford University Press, 1926.

_____.*Tribes of the Niger Delta: Their Religions and Customs.* London: The Sheldon Press, 1932.

Thompson, Robert Farris. "The Sign of the Divine King," *African Arts/Arts d'Afrique* vol. 3, no. 3 (Spring 1970), pp. 2–17, 74–80.
On Yoruba beaded crowns.

Torday, Emil. *Camp and Tramp in African Wilds.* London: Seeley, Service & Company, 1913.

_____.*On the Trail of the Bushongo.* London: Seeley, Service & Company, 1925. Reprinted: New York: Negro Universities Press, 1969.

_____,and T. A. Joyce. "Notes ethnographiques sur les peuples communément appelés Bakuba ainsi que sur les peuplades apparantées. Les Bushongo." *Annales du Musée du Congo Belge,* ser. 3, vol. 2, fasc. 1. Brussels: 1910.

Tyrrell, Barbara. *Tribal Peoples of Southern Africa.* Cape Town: Gothic Printing Company, 1968.

Verger, Pierre. *Congo Belge et Ruanda-Urundi.* Introduction by Charles D'Ydwalle. Paris: Paul Hartmann, 1925.
225 illustrations of the Mangbetu and others, showing hair-styling, beaded ornaments.

Verleyen, Emile. *Congo patrimonie de la Belgique.* Brussels: Editions de Visscher, 1950.
References to Pygmies, ornaments, hair-styling.

Ward, Herbert. *A Voice from the Congo.* New York: Scribner's, 1910.

The World Displayed; or A Curious Collection of Voyages and Travels, selected from the writers of all nations. In which the conjectures and interpolations of several vain editors and translators are expunged, every relation is made concise and plain and the divisions of countries and kingdoms are clearly and distinctly noted. 20 vols. London: J. Newberry at the Bible and Sun in St. Paul's Church-yard, 1759–1816.

JEWELRY

Daniel, F. "Bead workers of Ilorin, Nigeria," *Man,* vol. 37 (1937), p. 24.

DeNegri, Eve. "Jewelry," *Nigeria Magazine,* no. 74 (September 1962), pp. 42–54.

_____."The King's Beads," *Nigeria Magazine,* no. 82 (September 1964), pp. 210–216.

_____."Small Currency—Blue Shells and Manillas," *Nigeria Magazine,* no. 102 (September 1969), pp. 504–511.

Foote, H. S. "Gold Ornaments from Ashanti," *Cleveland Museum Bulletin,* vol. 31 (1944), pp. 180–181.

"Ivory Ornaments," *Nigeria Magazine,* no. 77 (1963), pp. 105–116.

Lystad, Robert A. *The Ashanti: A Proud People.* New Brunswick, N.J.: Rutgers University Press, 1958.
Discussion of Ashanti gold ornaments.

Meyerowitz, E. L. R. *The Akan of Ghana: Their Ancient Beliefs.* London: Faber and Faber, 1958.
Discussion of the ornaments of kingship.

Neher, Gerald. "Brass-Casting in North-East Nigeria," *Nigerian Field,* vol. 29 (January 1964), pp. 16–27.

Nzekwu, J. Onuora. "Ivory Ornaments in Onitsha," *Nigeria Magazine,* no. 77 (June 1963), pp. 105–116.

Plass, Margaret. *7 Metals of Africa.* Philadelphia: University of Pennsylvania Museum, 1959.

Shaw, C. T. "Bead-making with a Bow-Drill in the Gold Coast," *Journal of the Royal Anthropological Institute,* vol. 75 (1945), pp. 45–50.

Wild, R. P. "The Manufacture of a 'Ntiriba' Hairpin at Ohuasi, Ashanti," *Man,* vol. 39, no. 17 (1939), pp. 16–18.

TEXTILES

Barbour, Jane, and Doig Simmons, eds. *Adire Cloth in Nigeria.* Ibadan, Nigeria: University of Ibadan, Institute of African Studies, 1971.

Basden, G. T. *Among the Ibos of Nigeria.* Philadelphia: Lippincott, 1921.
Description of Ibo cloth.

Beauchamp, P. C. "A Gay Garb for Ghana," *West Africa,* vol. 41, no. 2081 (March 2, 1957), p. 209.
Cloth designs and techniques.

Boas, Franz. *Primitive Art.* New York: Dover, 1935.
Hausa embroidery and designs.

Boyer, Ruth. "Narrow Band Weaving among the Yorubas of Nigeria." *Craft Horizons,* vol. 24 (November-December 1964), pp. 28–29, 52–53.

Clarke, J. D. "The Use of Vegetable Dyes," *Nigeria Magazine,* no. 18 (1939), p. 158.

DeNegri, Eve. "Nigerian Textiles before Independence," *Nigeria Magazine,* no. 89 (June 1966), pp. 95–101.

Ene, J. Chunwike. "Indigenous Silk-Weaving in Nigeria," *Nigeria Magazine,* no. 81 (June 1964), pp. 127–136.

Gunn, Harold D. *A Handbook of the African Collections of the Commercial Museum.* Philadelphia: Museum of the Philadelphia Civic Center, n.d.
Description of textiles in permanent collection.

Hale, Sjarief. "Kente Cloth of Ghana," *African Arts,* vol. 3, no. 3 (Spring 1970), pp. 26–29.

Hambly, Wilfrid D. *The Ovimbundu of Angola.* Field Museum of Natural History Anthropological Series, vol. 21, no. 2, pp. 129–132. Chicago: 1934.

Harrell, Janet E. "Classifications and Documentation of the Eicher Collection of Selected Nigerian Textile Fabrics." Unpublished master's problem, Michigan State University, East Lansing, 1967.

Heathcote, David. "Hausa Embroidered Dress," *African Arts,* vol. 5, no. 2 (Winter 1972), pp. 12–19, 82–84.

Imperato, Pascal James, and Maril Shamir. "'Bokolanfini' Mud Cloth of the Bambara of Mali," *African Arts,* vol. 3, no. 4 (Summer 1970), pp. 32–41.

Kent, Kate P. *Introducing West African Cloth.* Denver: Denver Museum of Natural History, 1971.

Littlewood, Margaret. "Bamum and Bamileke," *Peoples of the Central Cameroons.* London: International African Institute, 1954.
Description of embroidery and beadwork.

MacCulloch, Merran. *The Peoples of Sierra Leone Protectorate.* London: International African Institute, 1950.

MacDonald, George. *The Gold Coast, Past and Present.* New York: Longmans, Green, 1898.
Description of looms, cloth, beads and beadwork.

Manoukian, Madeline. *The Akan and Ga-Adangme Peoples of the Gold Coast.* London: International African Institute, 1950.

Ojo, G. J. Afolabi. *Yoruba Culture: A Geographical Analysis.* London: University of London Press, 1966.
Description of dyeing, embroidery, weaving of cotton textiles.

Park, Mungo. *The Travels of Mungo Park.* London: J. M. Dent and Sons, 1907.
Description of cloth manufacture and leather tanning.

Plumer, Cheryl. *African Textiles: An Outline of Handcrafted Sub-Saharan Fabrics.* East Lansing: Michigan State University, 1970.

Polakoff, Claire. "The Art of Tie and Dye in Africa," *African Arts,* vol. 4, no. 3 (Spring 1971), pp. 28–80.

Saulawa, Mallam Iro. "Thread Making and Weaving in Katsina Province," *Nigeria Magazine,* no. 23 (1946), pp. 115–116.

Southern, A. E. "Cloth Making in Nigeria," *Nigeria Magazine,* no. 32 (1959), pp. 35–40.

Trowell, Margaret. *African Design.* 3rd ed. New York: Praeger, 1970.

Ukeje, L. O. "Weaving in Akwete," *Nigeria Magazine,* no. 74 (September 1963), pp. 32–41.

Vernon-Jackson, Hugh. "Craft Work in Bida," *Africa,* vol. 30 (January 1960), pp. 51–61.

Weeks, John. *Among the Primitive Bakongo.* Philadelphia: Lippincott, 1914. Reprinted: New York: Negro Universities Press, 1969.

Wenger, S., and H. Ulli Beier. "Adire—Yoruba Pattern Dyeing," *Nigeria Magazine,* no. 54 (1957), pp. 208–225.

MUSEUM ACCESSION NUMBERS

Where they exist, museum accession numbers for works illustrated are given below, grouped by museum and arranged in order of appearance within this volume.

AFRICAN COLLECTIONS, LINCOLN UNIVERSITY, PA.: p. 180 bottom, *Women's weave*, 9-056; p. 211, *Tied-and-dyed cloth*, 7-017. THE AMERICAN MUSEUM OF NATURAL HISTORY: p. 30, *Man's robe*, 90.2/2486; p. 34, *Drawstring breeches*, 90.1/7109; p. 35, *Drawstring breeches*, 90.1/9681; p. 38, *Man's robe*, 90.1/8511; p. 54, *Woman's apron*, 90.1/8876; p. 103 top, *Wooden ear plug*, 90.2/1849; p. 104, *Nose ornament*, 90.1/8315; p. 113 bottom, *Sweat scrapers*, 90.0/869, 870; 90.1/1031, 1035; p. 117, *Wooden comb*, 90.1/7915; p. 119 top, *Hairpins*, 90.2/5558–5562; p. 140, *Necklace*, 90.2/4150; p. 187, *Men's weave*, 90.2/1934; p. 191 top, *Men's weave*, 90.1/7173; p. 194, *Men's weave* (kente), 90.2/4950; p. 199, *Men's weave* (kente), 90.1/9409; pp. 202–203, 90.1/8616. THE BROOKLYN MUSEUM: p. 41, *Royal costume*, 22.1500, 1501; p. 62, *Beaded crown*, 70.109.1; p. 198, *Men's weave* (kente), 71.184. BUFFALO MUSEUM OF SCIENCE: p. 58, *Skirt or cape*, C 21623; p. 59, *Skirt or cape*, C 21625; p. 98, *Snuff bottle*, C 21615; p. 148 bottom, *Copper anklet*, 5066/C 14877. THE CLEVELAND MUSEUM: p. 134 top, *Brass neck ring*, G40.117; p. 137 top left, *Gold ring*, 51.320; p. 137 bottom right, *Gold soul disk*, 35.310. THE COLLEGE MUSEUM, HAMPTON INSTITUTE: pp. 36–37, *Drawstring breeches*, 209605; p. 64 bottom left, *Beaded hat*, 11.39; p. 88 right, *Ceremonial knife*, 15.226; p. 116, *Copper comb*, 11.76; p. 166, *Woman's raffia wraparound*, 11.180. FIELD MUSEUM OF NATURAL HISTORY: p. 42, *Appliquéd costume*, 221542; p. 81, *Fan*, 210291; p. 158, *Beaten bark cloth*, 210647; p. 159, *Beaten bark cloth*, 210129; p. 165, *Raffia cloth*, 34011; p. 186, *Men's weave*, 221659; p. 213, *Tied-and-dyed cloth*, 221668. INDIANA UNIVERSITY ART MUSEUM: p. 156, *Beaten bark cloth*, 63.327. R. H. LOWIE MUSEUM OF ANTHROPOLOGY: p. 12 top, *Cache-sexe*, 5-4236a; p. 100, *Labret*, 5-6791; p. 105, *Nose ornament*, 5-777; p. 112 middle, *Finger knives*, 5-6811, 5-6815; p. 139 right, *Necklace*, 5-839; p. 141 top, *Bead necklace*, 5-7336; p. 150, *Coiled-wire bangle*, 5-799C. MILWAUKEE PUBLIC MUSEUM: p. 44, *Dance costume*, 34449/4459; p. 106 top, *Earrings*, 36985/9486 a and b; p. 121, *Combs*, 7100/2676; 7102/2676, 2995; p. 139 left, *Necklace*, 36291/9486; p. 149 top, *Ivory bangle*, 39619/10672; p. 195, *Men's weave*, 57503/18521. MINNESOTA MUSEUM OF ART: p. 157 bottom, *Beaten bark cloth*, 63.07.02; p. 167, *Man's raffia wraparound (fragment)*, 63.03.42. MUSEUM OF AFRICAN ART: p. 60, *Cape or skirt*, 68-19-21. THE MUSEUM OF PRIMITIVE ART: p. 33, *Man's robe*, 65.67; p. 77, *Dance cap*, 60.179; p. 131 bottom left, *Gold pendant*, 65.11; p. 132, *Gold necklace*, 58.312; p. 137 top right, *Gold pendant*, 60.37; p. 151 top, *Wood armlet*, 58.211. THE PEABODY MUSEUM, HARVARD UNIVERSITY: p. 12 bottom, *Penis caps*, E 7932; E 15856, 7; E 22986; E 28800, 1; p. 72, *Coiled basketry hat*, H-1170; p. 118, *Bone comb*, 05-31-50/64980; p. 135 bottom, *Copper neck ring*, 46-78-50/6029; p. 142, *Waist ornament*, 29-76-50/H-995; p. 147 bottom, *Iron anklet*, 22-2-50/B-3401. THE PEABODY MUSEUM OF SALEM: p. 73, *War hat*, E 7010; p. 141 bottom, *Bead necklace*, E 25.788; p. 207 bottom, *Raffia skirt*, E 2317; p. 214, *Tied-and-dyed skirt*, E 20.169. ROYAL ONTARIO MUSEUM: p. 84 bottom, *Wooden sandals*, HAC 484, 485; p. 112 bottom, *Razor pin*, HA 560; p. 125 top, *Hairpins*, HA 578; HAC 115, 119 (ivory); HAC 114 (rattan); p. 125 bottom, *Ivory hairpin*, HA 1315. THE SMITHSONIAN INSTITUTION: p. 64 bottom right, *Hat*, 15073; p. 66, *Feather ornament*, 204463; p. 75, *Hat*, 249806. UNIVERSITY MUSEUM, PHILADELPHIA: p. 17, *Brass anklets*, 66.28.1; p. 55, *Woman's apron*, AF 3717; p. 79, *Hat*, 29.59.113; p. 102, *Snuff bottle*, AF 4233; p. 114, *Tweezers*, AF 2273, AF 2276; p. 134 middle, *Wooden neck ring*, 68.18.3; p. 134 bottom, *Copper pendant*, AF 894; p. 148 top, *Copper anklets*, AF 4747. UCLA MUSEUM OF CULTURAL HISTORY: p. 47, *War dress*, x70-127; p. 52 right, *Belt and waist ornament*, x65-5496; p. 78, *Hat*, 378-383; p. 85, *Boots*, x65-5797; p. 86, *Whisk*, x65-8521; p. 88 left, *Fan*, x65-5796; p. 112 top, *Razor pins*, 382-40/41/43; p. 115 left, *Ivory or bone comb*, x65-8506; p. 126 top, *Ivory necklace*, x67-881; p. 138, *Neckpiece*, 379-496; p. 144 top, *Gold object*, x65-8524; p. 192, *Men's weave*, x66-924. UNIVERSITY OF DENVER (Dept. of Anthropology): p. 177, *Women's weave*, DU 3711.

PHOTOGRAPH CREDITS

Field photographs courtesy Allison Davis, Chicago, 99; Anita J. Glaze, Champaign, Ill., 63 bottom, 83, 161 top; Barbara W. Merriam, Bloomington, Ind., 109, 126, 161 bottom; The Peabody Museum, Harvard University, Cambridge, Mass., 67; Roy Sieber, Bloomington, Ind., 18, 20, 160, 224; Francis Speed, Ife, Nigeria, 13, 21, 22; James Vaughan, Bloomington, Ind., 82; C. Zagourski, 14, 15, 91, 92. Reproductions from early travelers' accounts courtesy Lilly Library of Indiana University, Bloomington, 25 top, 25 bottom, 26, 51, 63 top, 87.

All other photographs have been supplied by the owners of the works reproduced, except in the following cases: African Museum Collections, Lincoln University, Pa., 154 bottom; Best Photographics, East Lansing, Mich., 171 top; Hillel Burger for The Peabody Museum, Cambridge, Mass., 118, 135 bottom, 147 bottom; Claude Conkling & Sons, Inc., Portland, Ore., 124 right; Larry Dupont, Los Angeles, 47, 78, 88 left, 112 top, 115 left, 136, 138, 144 top, 192; Delmar Lipp, Washington, D.C., 60, 143 bottom; Los Angeles County Museum of Art, 217; R. H. Lowie Museum of Anthropology, Berkeley, 169; James Mathews, New York, 36, 95, 96, 106 bottom, 115 right, 128, 129 bottom, 131 top right, 145, 147 top, 153 top left, 154 top, 158, 159, 165, 168 bottom, 186, 191 bottom, 200, 213; Uldis Saule, Evanston, Ill., 84 top, 162, 164, 206 top; John Simmons, Nashville, Tenn., 32, 157 top, 171 bottom, 179; Richard Stewart, University of Delaware, Newark, 71, 108, 149 bottom; M. Swalling, Learning Resources/Photographic Services, University of California, Santa Barbara, 175 top; Frank J. Thomas, Los Angeles, 39, 48, 49, 52 right, 56, 57, 68, 69, 70, 85, 86, 103 bottom, 119 bottom, 124 left, 126 top, 129 top, 130, 131 bottom right, 133, 137 bottom left, 143 top, 144 bottom, 151 bottom, 152 both, 153 bottom right, 180 top, 184, 185, 188, 204, 206 bottom, 208, 212, 215, 220, 222, 225; Charles Uht, New York, 33, 77, 131 bottom right, 132, 137 top right, 151 top; University of Washington Audio-Visual Production Services, Seattle, 50, 189.